AN INTRODUCTION TO NON-POLICY DEBATING

Joseph Corcoran

California State University,

Chico

 KENDALL/HUNT PUBLISHING COMPANY
2460 Kerper Boulevard P.O. Box 539 Dubuque, Iowa 52004-0539

To Frank Corcoran, a man who never lost an argument.

This edition has been printed directly from camera-ready copy.

Copyright © 1988 by Kendall/Hunt Publishing Company

ISBN 0-8403-6522-5

Printed in the United States of America
10 9 8 7 6 5 4

4. Additional Principles 37

5. Using Sound Reasoning 51

Contents

Preface

Over the past two decades, non-policy debate has overtaken policy debate as the predominant intercollegiate activity. In 1975, the Cross Examination Debate Association (C.E.D.A.) developed the use of national non-policy debate topics. Since then, C.E.D.A. has risen to a current membership level of approximately 300 universities and colleges. Unfortunately, this relatively new activity lacks the concrete refinement of its predecessor. The problem is that non-policy debate's practice has preceded its theory. The development of a coherent, comprehensive theory of non-policy argumentation is still in the process of development. With such a newborn theory, there exists much disagreement and some confusion among scholars and participants. Brey (1989) argues, "CEDA has emerged as a competitive means of argumentation without a firm theoretical foundation." However, the real problem is with the participants, who actually have to debate in front of critics and instructors. One scholar states, "Despite the increase of non-policy debating, little has been written to offer direction to the participants in the activity (Brownlee, 1980)." Obviously, the lack of a comprehensive guide for students creates a grave problem for argumentation instructors and debate coaches, as well as for students themselves. The purpose of this book is to help fill the void in the literature by providing the beginning debate student with an instructional manual in non-policy debate.

Usually, non-policy debates dispute the nature and application of values (values such as freedom and the sanctity of human life). This manual supplies college-level argumentation students and intercollegiate debate competitors with a written text for helping them understand the concepts of non-policy debate. This book also describes the uses and tests of sound reasoning and, by doing so, serves as a good beginning text for argumentation classes or as a general guidebook for forensic teams. As a text for argumentation students, it can allow for a fuller understanding of classroom assignments and a smoother transition into intercollegiate debating if so desired. As a required reading for forensic students, it may save a coaching staff or a senior debater endless hours of explanation and instruction. Additional coaching time then may be spent developing specific arguments and necessary skills. In its seven chapters, this text addresses fundamentals, affirmative and negative approaches, special problems of non-policy argumentation, sound vs. fallacious reasoning, and quasi-policy debating.

As colleges and universities across the country increase critical-thinking curricula, thousands of general-education students are enrolling in argumentation and debate courses as a palatable way of fulfilling their critical-thinking requirements. This manual will help fill the void in the literature and help students learn valuable critical thinking skills. Ehninger and Brockriede (1963, p. 3), write, "A critical decision is more reliable than a decision that is arrived at uncritically, because [a critical decision] is based on a careful study of pertinent evidence and values." Non-policy theory has begun to unlock the mysteries of understanding values, which play such a large part in the debate activity and in critical thinking

A final rationale is that non-policy debate offers a wider range of argumentation than does its counterpart, policy debate. The latter attempts to resolve policy or legislative-type decisions. However, there are many controversies in the world which are not legislative. People contend over values, beliefs, and facts, as well as policies. In fact, much of what people argue about concerns what to believe as well as what to do. For example, before a woman chooses whether to have an abortion (a policy decision), she probably has to decide whether abortion is good or bad, moral or immoral (a value decision). Many non-policy resolutions address just that type of value controversy.

I would like to acknowledge Dr. Steven R. Brydon, Dr. Isaac E. Catt, Dr. Suzanne Larson, and Dr. William Todd-Mancillas. The instruction I received from each of them was instrumental in the completion of this book.

1| FUNDAMENTALS

EDUCATIONAL DEBATE

Educational debate is a highly structured competition between individuals (Lincoln/Douglas Debate) or two-person teams (Team Debate). A typical debate round lasts anywhere from one hour to two hours, depending on time constraints and format. College debaters need to be prepared to debate both the affirmative and negative sides of a resolution. A resolution, the focus of a debate, is a declarative statement of fact, value, or policy, worded in unbiased terms. An example of a non-policy resolution is "Resolved: That the American judicial system has overemphasized freedom of the press." An affirmative advocate or team would support that resolution; the negative side would refute the affirmative's case. Table 1 lists the different time constraints for speakers in each of the different types of debate. As you will note, in team debate each speaker gives one constructive speech and one rebuttal speech. In Lincoln/Douglas (LD) debate, the same is true except that the affirmative speaker gives two rebuttal speeches to compensate for the longer negative constructive (12 minutes). The main purpose of a constructive speech is to build arguments. The main purpose of a rebuttal speech is to refute an opponent's arguments and rebuild your original ones.

Finally, debate is a contest that is judged by an impartial third party. In intercollegiate competition, that third party is usually a forensics coach, a speech communication professor, or a graduate student. In the argumentation classroom, that third party is the instructor. Most critics, as well as debaters, take comprehensive notes on what are called flow-sheets. Normally, a flow-sheet is nothing more than a legal-sized piece of paper turned sideways with each of the speeches in the debate written in shorthand in columns side by side, starting with the first affirmative constructive (1AC) and ending with the second affirmative rebuttal (2AR). The critic evaluates the debate based on those notes. A failure to respond to an argument appears as a blank spot on the flow-sheet corresponding to the speaker who is guilty of "dropping" the argument. Usually, a failure to respond results in an opponents' advantage on that particular issue. The critic also evaluates his or her notes to see which debater or team had better reasoning, analysis, and evidence on each of the other issues in the debate. The debater or team that he or she feels did the better job of debating wins the debate.

1

TABLE 1
Traditional Speaking Order and Time Constraints

C.E.D.A.			L/D C.E.D.A.			N.D.T.		
1AC	8	minutes	1AC	8	minutes	1AC	10	minutes
c/x	3	minutes	c/x	3	minutes	c/x	3	minutes
1NC	8	minutes	1NC	12	minutes	1NC	10	minutes
c/x	3	minutes	c/x	3	minutes	c/x	3	minutes
2AC	8	minutes				2AC	10	minutes
c/x	3	minutes				c/x	3	minutes
2NC	8	minutes				2NC	10	minutes
c/x	3	minutes				c/x	3	minutes
1NR	4	minutes				1NR	5	minutes
1AR	4	minutes	1AR	6	minutes	1AR	5	minutes
2NR	4	minutes	1NR	6	minutes	2NR	5	minutes
2AR	4	minutes	2AR	4	minutes	2AR	5	minutes

KEY

A C Affirmative Constr.	1__ First
N C Negative Constructive	2__ Second
N R Negative Rebuttal	c/x Cross Examination
A R Affirmative Rebuttal	L/D Lincoln/Douglas

BENEFITS OF DEBATE

In the academic world, few activities compare to debate in terms of academic and personal benefits. A serious debate student acquires skills in critical thinking, research, speaking, organization, writing, cross examination, critical listening, and leadership. The student also learns the theory and practice of argumentation and debate, a body of knowledge that has application in nearly every field of inquiry and employment.

In fact, debate as a scholastic activity has been heralded as effective training for aspirants in all fields. The prospective business-person learns how to advocate an idea, just as he or she will do at corporate board meetings. The aspiring teacher learns to prepare notes and deliver well-documented speeches on the spur of the moment, a skill that will pay for itself over and over again when preparing future lectures for the classroom. The hopeful lawyer learns to prepare briefs, practice cross examination, and (depending on the debate topic) perhaps even do some legal research. The aspiring scientist, architect, or computer scientist learn communication skills that will give them an edge over their colleagues in the job interview process. In addition, those skills will help bridge the gap between the technological and the lay world. The list of potential benefits is endless. A student with communication skills has a definite edge over his or her colleague who lacks those skills. Helen Wise, the former president of the National Education Association, explains,

> No college freshman can project twenty five years to decide what he needs to learn--subject matter is easily forgotten and in today's world, the knowledge explosion makes constant learning an inevitability. But all adults today need to be able to communicate with clarity, to articulate ideas, to reason, to separate key facts from the barrage of ideas we all are exposed to every day.

> No single activity can prepare one better than debating--the ability to think on one's feet, to form conclusions rapidly, to answer questions logically and with clarity, to summarize ideas are all processes which forensic (speech and debate) activities develop and develop well (Freeley, 1986, p.13).

As Dr. Wise tells us, debate is the best preparation for anyone's future, no matter what it will be. Therefore, any student interested in the best preparation for his or her future ought to think seriously about participating in debate.

REASONS FOR COMPETING

There are many reasons for students to compete in non-policy debate. First, as currently practiced, intercollegiate non-policy debate is easier for the novice or beginning student. The Cross Examination Debate Association (C.E.D.A.), the intercollegiate organization that sponsors non-policy debate, began in 1971 with a philosophy of making debate more accessible to all students. C.E.D.A. started as a reaction to National Debate Tournament (N.D.T.) debate, a type of debate that encourages extremely rapid rates of speaking and extensive researching of the topic. N.D.T. debate emphasizes the content of the message. There are many benefits to debating N.D.T., but accessibility of the beginner is not one of them. C.E.D.A., on the other hand, took the emphasis off of rapid speaking and extensive research and asked its competitors to be more communicative instead. Rather than look at debate as an activity with emphasis on content, C.E.D.A. chose to view debate as an activity with emphasis on public speaking. Novice C.E.D.A. competitors do not have to spend as much time as their N.D.T. counterparts researching the topic or learning to speak rapidly. That does not mean that research and delivery are not important. C.E.D.A. debaters certainly spend time practicing and researching, and good senior division C.E.D.A. teams probably spend as much time as their N.D.T. colleagues at the two activities. However, to start in C.E.D.A. does not require as much skill or preparation. Some argumentation scholars have even proposed that the nature of the non-policy resolution lends itself to greater accessibility.

As a matter of fact, C.E.D.A. has grown to become the largest debate organization in the country. In the Spring of 1975, C.E.D.A. institutionalized non-policy topics. Since then, membership in the organization has risen to a current level of approximately 300 colleges and universities. As shown, the first advantage of non-policy debating, accessibility, seems to be quantitatively verifiable.

A second advantage of non-policy debate is that it offers a wider range of argumentation. Policy debate attempts to resolve policy or legislative controversies. However, there are many controversies in the world which are not legislative. People contend over values, beliefs, and facts, as well as policies. In fact, much of what people argue about concerns what to believe rather than what to do. After all, before one can decide what action to take, often he or she needs to know what to believe. For example, before a woman chooses whether to have an abortion (a policy decision), she probably has to decide whether abortion is good or bad, moral or immoral (a value decision). Many non-policy resolutions address just that type of value controversy.

A third advantage of non-policy debate is that it is a relatively new area of inquiry. Theory, as well as practice, has evolved rapidly. Students and coaches involved in the activity have shaped its future. Students of today can have a similar impact on the development of the activity. Debate coaches and argumentation scholars (not that the two are mutually exclusive) often ask students to employ a new development in theory. Or, more probably, argumentation scholars write into theory what they see working in practice. Therefore, a serious debate student can help shape the future of non-policy debate.

THE PURPOSE OF THIS BOOK

While non-policy theory has developed rapidly, few people have attempted to consolidate the information into a digestible form for the beginning debate student. In addition, there are many controversies in the literature. This manual does not attempt to resolve those controversies, but rather to identify them and offer practical advice to students. The purpose of this manual, then, is to serve as a guide for the beginning non-policy debater. Much of non-policy theory has been written by people with a great knowledge of argumentation and extensive experience at coaching, but without ever having competed in the activity. This book represents the culmination of a decade of non-policy debate participation and coaching. Coming at the activity from a practical standpoint, hopefully the advice contained in this manual can be of service to the novice competitor who desires answers to questions.

DEFINITION OF NON-POLICY DEBATE

In order to understand non-policy debate, a moderate understanding of policy debate is important. Policy debate asks the advocates to debate whether a specific change in the present system (of government, of education, of foreign policy) is necessary. Change always involves a certain amount of risk. In order to compensate for that risk, the affirmative side is asked to prove a number of contingent factors. Those factors are called **stock issues**. In policy debate, the stock issues fall basically into two categories: justification and plan. Justification is the requirement to prove that a need to change exits. The justification stock issues are harm, inherency, and significance. Harm refers to the advocates' burden to prove that the *status quo* (the present system) is flawed, usually by showing that people are harmed through injury, death, or loss of money or property. The second justification issue is that of inherency. The inherency requirement asks the debaters to prove that the *status quo* is to blame for the harm. They can do that by showing that either the structure of the present system (structural inherency) or the attitude of the people (attitudinal inherency) have caused the problem or prevented its resolution. Inherency can mean, at the simplest level, the causes of the problem. For example, one may argue that an inherent reason why women are still discriminated against in the job market is because of people's attitudes (attitudinal inherency). A third justification issue is significance. Any harm must be quantitatively significant in order to justify a major change in the *status quo*. For example, if only one person dies of a certain toxic chemical, federal control of that chemical may be difficult to justify. One person's death does not usually provide the quantitative significance required. However, if thousands are killed and tens of thousands injured by the chemical, one has a stronger case that something be done. Harm, inherency, and significance all must be proven before an affirmative debater can hope to win. Failing to prove one of those factors may result in an affirmative loss, depending on the critic and the negative refutation.

Equally important for the advocate to demonstrate are the plan stock issues: workability, solvency, and advantages. A plan is a concrete, specific proposal that serves as an example of the proposition. Usually, a plan will spell out the agency that will administer the program. That agency could be an existing agency, such as the Environmental Protection Agency, or it could be a new agency created for the purposes of debate. Furthermore, the plan usually spells out the mandates, the enforcement mechanism, and the plan's funding. Workability refers to the technical aspects of the plan, whether they can work. For plans advocating a new law, often workability issues deal with enforcement. For example, workability problems arise in an affirmative plan mandating that all citizens must volunteer to have their cars inspected for safety flaws (Freeley, 1986). The plan would not work simply because people would not volunteer to have their cars inspected if it could mean mandated and expensive repairs. A second plan stock issue is solvency. Solvency, as the word implies, refers to whether the plan actually solves the problem that was outlined in the justification section. Solvency, as discussed later, can have application in non-policy debate as well. A final plan stock issue is advantages. Usually, the affirmative and the negative battle over the issue of advantages. The affirmative has to prove that the advantages of the plan outweigh the disadvantages that the negative argues. In addition, the advantages have to be accrued directly and uniquely from the topical aspects of the plan. They cannot be derived from anything else. An affirmative that is able to prove and win all six of these issues will usually win the debate.

Having briefly discussed policy debate, non-policy debate should be easier to understand. While policy debate advocates a change in the structure of the *status quo*, non-policy debate usually evaluates the relative value (good or bad, beneficial or detrimental) of something. Non-policy debate, as the negating prefix indicates, is everything outside the realm of policy debate, at least theoretically. Consequently, the non-policy stock issues are much different from the policy stock issues. The stock issues for non-policy debate are twofold: definitive and designative. The definitive stock issue is divided into two parts. The first part involves defining the terms of the resolution. In policy debate the terms of the resolution are usually operationally defined through the presentation of the plan's implementation. In non-policy debate, that is not possible because there is no need to present a plan in order to justify the resolution. The team or advocate affirming the non-policy proposition, therefore, needs to explicitly define the terms of the resolution, at least the critical terms. The second subdivision of the definitive stock issue is the presentation of a criteria for judging the debate round. A criteria can be a goal, a standard, a value, or the conclusion to a philosophical treatise. Usually the criteria is on a higher level of abstraction than the proposition itself. For instance, a criteria often deals with economic, social, or political values. The criteria is used to measure the extent of benefit or detriment asked for by the resolution. In other words, a criterion is like a litmus test.

The second stock issue in non-policy debate is the designative stock issue. This stock issue simply involves the application of the criteria to a specific case. For example, one debating the proposition, "Resolved: That illegal immigration into the United States is seriously detrimental to the United States," might use a social value, such as the lack of crime, as the criterion. In the application, one might prove that illegal immigrants are significant contributors to crime in the U.S. Or, on the same topic, one might offer a political value as a criterion: full employment for U.S. citizens. By applying that criterion, one might find that illegal immigrants take jobs that Americans want. If the job displacement is widespread, it could be significant enough to justify the "seriously detrimental" phrase in the resolution. Regardless of the actual application, more and more debate critics are requiring that affirmatives show that their application is significant. For instance, if illegal immigrants only contributed to a fraction of one percent of the crime in the U.S., then even though the criterion was applied successfully, the small amount of crime does not justify the resolution. Of course, if the affirmative could prove that the small amount of crime is significant (e.g. many illegal immigrants are potential presidential assassins), then it may be debatable.

CLASSIFICATION OF NON-POLICY TOPICS

The two stock issues for non-policy debate, as shown, are the definitive and the designative stock issues. Using those stock issues is sometimes complicated by the diversity of the types of non-policy propositions. The most useful classification to date was developed by Dixon and Leslie (1984). They argue that C.E.D.A. topics since 1975 have concerned one of three areas: fact, value, and quasi-policy. This categorization simply adds one more division to the original fact, value, policy division (see Table 2). Table 2 demonstrates the relationship between the four basic types of propositions. In order to prove a proposition of value, one needs to have already established fact. Similarly, in order to prove a policy, one needs to have already proven both fact and value. Everything preceding policy on this continuum can be considered a non-policy proposition. As a consequence, non-policy propositions which rank closer to fact on the continuum may have requirements similar to proving stock issues of fact. In addition, non-policy resolutions which rank closer to policy may have some requirements similar to policy requirements. The importance of this distinction is that, when debating one of the three types of non-policy topics (fact, value, and quasi-policy), the debater must adjust his or her strategy accordingly.

TABLE 2
Hierarchical Order of Propositions

Non-Policy Propositions	Policy Propositions
	POLICY
QUASI-POLICY	
VALUE	
FACT	

Fact

Factual propositions ask advocates to determine the truth or falsehood of the statement. An example of a factual proposition might be, "Resolved: That JFK was killed by a political conspiracy." Debating that topic would require fulfilling the stock issues for factual debates: Who, what, where, when, how, and why; or, in legal terms, suspect (who), crime (what), opportunity (where, when), means (how), and motive (why). An example of a factual resolution is the Spring 1982 C.E.D.A. topic, which reads,

"Resolved: That the American judicial system has overemphasized the rights of the accused." Debaters were asked to determine, in fact, whether our judicial system did too much for the accused. Implied in that factual determination is that the judicial system should never overemphasize anything because overemphasis is always harmful. Yet, the resolution did not say anything about harm or benefit, as the typical value resolution would. Technically, an affirmative could have argued that we benefit from the judicial system's preferential treatment of those accused of crimes.

Another example of a proposition of fact is the Spring 1983 C.E.D.A. topic, which reads, "Resolved: That individual rights of privacy are more important than any other Constitutional right." Affirmatives had a difficult time defending that statement. In elimination rounds, almost no one chose to debate the affirmative when given the choice. The problem lay perhaps in the categorization of the topic. Most teams approached the topic as though it were a value resolution. However, the topic does not necessarily ask for an evaluation. It may be merely asking for facts about how our court system deals with rights of privacy. At the San Francisco State Attorney Judged Tournament that year, a Humboldt State team, coached by Suzanne Larson, ran a case that argued that resolution as a factual proposition. Their case thesis was that whenever the Supreme Court recognized a right of privacy, it was always more important than any other right. The nature of the right of privacy made it that way. The right of privacy is not spelled out in the Bill of Rights, but is only implied. Their case was a factual determination based on the Supreme Court's record. Of course, there are some good arguments against Humboldt's case. Nevertheless, their team won the tournament even though it was locked in affirmative in both semi-finals and finals. Correct classification of the topic as a proposition of fact, therefore, can help determine victory or defeat.

Value

A second type of non-policy proposition is the value proposition. A value topic evaluates something other than a suggested policy. A value proposition proposes that something is either good or bad. This category tends to be the more general of the non-policy topics. In fact, the term, value debate, is often used synonymously with the term, non-policy debate. As a rule of thumb, if a topic does not seem to fit into the other two categories, it probably should be classified as a value topic.

An example of a value topic is the Spring 1981 C.E.D.A. topic, which reads, "Resolved: That activism in politics by religious groups harms the American political process." In this topic, the debater is simply asked to determine the "value" of religious activism: Is it harmful or beneficial to the political process?

A subdivision of the value classification that is important to mention is the comparative-value resolution. In this type of resolution, two things are compared to each other to determine which has more "value" than the other. An example of this type of value resolution is the 1980 Fall C.E.D.A. topic, which advocates, "Resolved: That protection of the national environment is a more important goal than satisfaction of American energy demands." With this type of proposition, the advocate must establish a hierarchy of values. A value or criterion to support the environment might be the health of humans. The affirmative, debating the above proposition, would have to prove that health is more important than production or transportation, values of meeting energy demands. Thus, the proposition's proponents would be establishing the hierarchy of health over production or health over transportation. This type of topic presents many problems for affirmative debaters because they are asked to evaluate the relative worth of two things, instead of one.

Quasi-Policy

Some argumentation scholars have defined a quasi-policy topic as one which evaluates a present or suggested policy. However, the inclusion of present policies in that definition blurs the line between value and quasi-policy topics. A more accurate definition of a quasi-policy topic is *a topic which evaluates a suggested policy*. For example, the 1982 Fall C.E.D.A. topic reads, "Resolved: That a unilateral freeze by the United States on the production and development of nuclear weapons would be desirable." Note that the U.S. did not freeze nuclear weapon building in 1982; therefore, this topic fits the definition of *suggested*, rather than *present* policy evaluation. In this topic, advocates were asked to debate the relative worth of a future (suggested) policy, a unilateral freeze. Obviously, this type of non-policy topic may have some policy applications, such as arguing solvency, but that will be discussed at length later in the text.

The three classifications of non-policy propositions discussed here are not sacrosanct. They simply provide the simplest approach for the beginning C.E.D.A. or non-policy debater. Additionally, these three divisions, fact, value, and quasi-policy, allow for practical approaches for both affirmatives and negatives.

SUMMARY

In the first chapter of this manual, the definition and importance of debate, especially non-policy debate, was discussed. Additionally, the classification of non-policy topics was illustrated. Hopefully, now the reader has a better understanding of non-policy debate. In the ensuing chapters, this manual will address affirmative approaches to non-policy debate (chapter 2), negative approaches to non-policy debate (chapter 3), additional concepts in non-policy debate (chapter 4), and sound vs. fallacious reasoning (chapters 5 and 6). The beginning debate student will learn how to develop and write a non-policy debate case. He or she will learn how to approach the negative position. The novice also will learn some suggested ways to handle difficult situations, such as presumption shifts and definitional arguments. Finally, chapter five and six outline strategies for using sound logic and explain methods for exposing opponent's fallacious reasoning.

2| AFFIRMATIVE

THE AFFIRMATIVE CASE

In order to debate the affirmative side of a topic, debaters need to prepare an eight-minute presentation, called an affirmative case. The first affirmative speaker makes that presentation as the first order of business in a debate. An affirmative case in non-policy debate is a highly structured argument, fulfilling both the definitive and the designative stock issues. By highly structured is meant that the first affirmative speaker actually speaks in outline form. For instance, he or she actually says things like, "contention one, military support is necessary to prevent Iraqi expansion; sub-point A, Iraq is expansionistic." Exactly how to substructure a case is discussed later in this chapter. A typical case is divided into three separate parts: definition of terms (definitive stock issue), criteria (definitive stock issue), and application of the criteria (designative stock issue). Additionally, an affirmative case needs to have anywhere from ten to twenty quotations, with full source citation, included in the text. Therefore, writing a good case often involves doing a sufficient amount of research first. This chapter will first look at how to research and analyze a topic, second how to write an affirmative case, and third how to prepare second affirmative constructive.

RESEARCHING AND ANALYZING THE TOPIC

Often, the novice debater should begin by sitting down with his or her experienced colleagues and coaches to analyze the topic. Discuss what the topic means and what some possible research angles might be. After you get a basic conception, you then need to do some background research on the topic. It is always helpful to have some background knowledge before brainstorming possible affirmative cases.

Start your research in the more general indexes in the library. Go to the card catalogue and *The Readers Guide to Periodical Literature*. Try to find a general book or article on the subject. Read it to get a better feel for the topic. Another good start with research is to interview one of the professors at your college. Professors are usually good at giving you leads for research and at giving you some general knowledge on the topic. Unfortunately, you cannot quote interviews in debate rounds. The information presented in debates must be available to all participants in the form of books, papers, articles, and the like. Once you have some general leads on the topic, it is then necessary to do some specific research.

The type of topic determines the best place to begin specific research. If it is a legal topic, such as the rights of privacy or the freedom of the press, the best place to start is the index to legal periodicals. If your university's library has a scant number of legal periodicals, you may need to go to a law library. On the two topics mentioned above, schools without access to legal periodicals took research trips to law libraries in order to accumulate the necessary amount of research. If it is a political topic, such as the nuclear freeze topic or the illegal immigration topic, the best place to begin specific research is in the U.S. documents section of the library. There is at least one government depository per congressional district. If your college is not a depository, try to go to the library in your district that is. Use either *The Monthly Catalogue* or *The Congressional Information Service* (CIS). Both of these have indexes and abstracts to help you locate necessary material. If you use government documents, the best source of information are the congressional hearings. A current hearing, within the last two years, can offer a plethora of sources for your debate file. Congressional hearings record the testimony of experts on a given subject. That testimony serves as extremely valuable debate evidence, for it is the same testimony upon which our government bases its major policy decisions. Furthermore, a typical hearing lasts for days and records testimony from hundreds of experts. A single hearing may be the source of enough debate evidence for an entire affirmative case. And, surprisingly, the government is usually pretty good at finding the best experts. Looking up the experts' names in other indexes, such as the card catalogue, can yield excellent results. Additionally, other government documents, such as *The Department of State Bulletin* or *The Congressional Quarterly Weekly Report*, are excellent sources for beginning research on a political topic. *The Congressional Record*, the verbatim account of debates and speeches in the House and Senate, is also a valuable source of political as well as social information. *The Congressional Record* has its own indexing system and can be located in the documents section of the library as well.

If the topic is one that the media have covered extensively, the best place to begin extensive research is with those media. *The Readers Guide to Periodical Literature* indexes the major news magazines (such as *Time* and *Newsweek*) which are frequently cited in non-policy debate rounds. Newspaper indexes can also access the print media. The country's major newspapers, such as *The Wall Street Journal, The Christian Science Monitor*, and *The Washington Post,* all have separate indexes that list articles by topic. Most college libraries carry at least a couple of these major newspapers and indexes.

Finally, if a topic is a specialized topic, such as education, then it behooves you to look in a related index, such as *The Educational Index.* While indexes are important tools to help locate information, many times simply going to a related magazine or newspaper on the shelf can yield fantastic results. Furthermore, indexes are usually at least a few months behind. Since recency of evidence is important in debate, great benefits can be gained from going straight to the shelf. Skimming through the contents pages of current issues of *The Bulletin of Atomic Scientist*, for instance, served as a productive short-cut during the nuclear freeze topic. A similar short-cut involves the card catalogue. A topic will usually have a certain set or sets of call numbers. All the related books on the subject can usually be found within the space of a few shelves or aisles. Simply looking through the newer books on those shelves can be a helpful short-cut.

Another angle worth pursuing, although it can be somewhat costly, is a computer search. Many libraries have hook ups to the major data bases in the country. If you approach the search correctly, your search can yield an immense amount of information. You might even check with your debate coach or instructor to see if your school's debate team would be willing to finance an extensive computer search on the national non-policy C.E.D.A. topic.

What do you do with the information once you find it? The first thing that you need to do is to read a good deal of the information just to get the gist of the subject matter. Some debate topics are a bit complicated. Without some fundamental knowledge of the way things work, it is fairly difficult to construct a convincing case. For example, beginning debaters had a difficult time with the United Nations topic until they gained a fundamental knowledge about how the United Nations worked. A second step is to begin looking for general arguments that support the proposition. Keep track of as many general arguments as you find. Often, your first attempts at listing those arguments may be a little disjointed. For example, were you doing research for the nuclear freeze resolution, you may list the following arguments: The world feels threatened, the U.S. has a superior nuclear arsenal, advancing technology causes a hair-trigger situation, *etc.* . . . Sometimes it is even difficult to determine whether an argument should be affirmative or negative. Don't worry; just list as many arguments as you find. Keep track of where in the magazines, documents, and books you found support for each of these arguments. Once you have made a list, get together with your colleagues to discuss them.

Once you begin to analyze the topic, the best thing to do is to brainstorm case ideas. Simply list, without evaluating, all the possible ideas you can think of based on your research. Once you have as many ideas as possible listed, then go through each one and evaluate it. Keep in mind the evaluative phrase in the resolution. That will give you a clue as to what you should be looking for. For example, if the resolution's evaluative phrase says, "is beneficial," then look for information pointing to possible benefits. On the other hand, if the proposition's evaluative phrase says, "is detrimental," then you should look for information that points to some kind of detriment.

Once you have listed possible cases and begun to evaluate them, try to classify the resolution at hand as either fact, value, or quasi-policy. This will give you insight as to the best approach to take. Remember, if the resolution is a factual resolution, then, look for information that demonstrates the truth of the resolution. If the resolution is a value resolution, which most non-policy topics are, then, search for information which supports the evaluative phrase in the resolution, e.g. "is beneficial." And, finally, if the resolution is quasi-policy, you, then, need to look for general arguments as to why the suggested policy is needed to solve the current problem(s). Be sure that the evidence that you find for your case is not conclusionary. Conclusionary or "blurb" evidence is evidence that states a conclusion without giving the analysis on which that conclusion should be based. For instance, a blurb piece of evidence may read that "the United Nations is no longer serving its original purpose" or "illegal immigration leads to other more serious crimes." Neither of these two statements explain why what they say is true and therefore are conclusionary. Be sure that the evidence that you use has sufficient analysis to stand on its own. A fairly good piece of evidence, taken from the religious activism topic, reads, "It is true that much, but certainly not all anti-abortion agitation arises from religious conviction . . . However, in the early days of the (abolitionists') struggle, abolitionists were largely a religiously grounded minority. Much of the civil rights movement in America grew out of the churches" (Goetz, 1980, p. 39). This evidence helps establish some of the "good" results of religious activism, emancipation of the slaves and the constitutional amendment for civil rights. Be sure also that your evidence is not from biased sources, but from credible sources. Once you have decided upon the case concept and have secured enough evidence, you are ready to write your affirmative case.

Remember that researching is a continuous process. Every good debater will continuously investigate the topic in order to improve the affirmative case and other significant arguments. Try to develop a system of finding a certain number of quotations daily or weekly. It's much easier to keep up with new developments on a debate topic a little at a time, than to try to do it all at once.

HOW TO WRITE A NON-POLICY AFFIRMATIVE CASE

Definition of Terms

As indicated earlier, a non-policy affirmative case is usually broken down into three separate sections. The definitive stock issue includes two of those sections: the definition of terms and the criteria for the case. The third section involves the designative stock issue, which is the application of the criteria. First, you need to find adequate definitions for the key terms of the resolution. Defining the terms correctly can have a direct bearing on whether you win or lose a debate round. C.E.D.A. and non-policy debate encourage debaters to take middle-of-the-road approaches to the topic. Jack Howe (1985) writes that debaters should "explore the main issues of a problem and not the peripheral ones" (p. 20). On the whole, most coaches view the non-policy resolution as a generalization, a statement that needs to be proven probably true in total. Taking one atypical example, although gaining more popularity, is usually frowned upon in C.E.D.A. Therefore, the novice debater should not try to be tricky by defining terms of the resolution in obscure ways. Look at the historical context of the resolution. Usually, debate topics concern contemporary controversies. The controversy as dealt with by the major media is usually the best hint as to how to analyze the resolution, and, hence, define its terms.

Topicality also becomes an issue when defining terms. The affirmative is required to be topical, *i.e.* discuss the resolution and not go beyond it. If the affirmative goes outside of the resolution, it will lose the debate if the negative can adequately prove that the affirmative is non-topical or non-resolutional. It is only logical that no matter how good an affirmative's arguments are, if they do not support the resolution, an affirmative cannot win the debate. There is some controversy over topicality in C.E.D.A. and non-policy debate, and that controversy will be addressed in the next chapter. As a beginning debater, it is only important to understand the concept of topicality and to try to use definitions that will guarantee the topicality of your presentation. Some judges will not base their decision on whether the affirmative is topical, but that is not a chance a beginning debater should take.

There are many ways to define terms for a debate. The most accepted way is to use a dictionary definition. A simple *Websters* or *Oxford English* definition is fine for most purposes. After a brief introduction (usually a serious quotation or humorous anecdote) and a verbatim reading of the resolution, simply list the key terms of the resolution with their dictionary definitions. (See the sample case in appendix "A.") Key terms usually involve words that may bring controversy. Obviously, words, such as "a" and "the," usually do not need to be defined. More and more, however, debaters are finding the need to define the various forms of the verb, "to be," such as "is." Often, the time-frame of the resolution becomes an issue. For instance, should one be able to argue past or future harms if the resolution says "is detrimental"? That is an issue that needs to be resolved by the debaters during the debate, starting with the first affirmative. It is also important to realize that many critics will not allow a team to define a term after their first speech. Therefore, if there is any question at all that a term's definition may become an issue, the term should be defined in the 1AC. 2AC is too late. Besides ordinary dictionaries, there are dictionaries for almost every profession and subject area: journalism, law, politics, language, philosophy, *etc.* . . . Using those dictionaries can be a valuable asset. For instance, on the media-coverage-of-terrorism topic, journalism dictionaries helped immensely in finding just the right definition. A note of caution, though, is that you should avoid using a certain type of dictionary unless it truly applies to the topic at hand. A common practice in C.E.D.A. currently is to use legal dictionaries for everything. That is not wise since law is an entity unto itself, and some law dictionaries and legal decisions even warn against cross-application to other professions and subjects. If the topic is a legal topic or if a word in the resolution has a legal connotation, then, by all means, use legal dictionaries. Simply, be cautioned not to misuse them.

While dictionary definitions are the most common, there are other ways to define terms. If the resolution is a quasi-policy topic it may be appropriate to define the "policy" terms of the resolution operationally. In other words, if the "policy" terms of the resolution suggest the policy of "a unilateral freeze," then it is often enough to simply state how you use that phrase in your speech. For example, you may want to define a unilateral freeze as a temporary challenge to the rest of the world or you may want to define it as a permanent freeze. Nowhere in a dictionary will you find either of those definitions. Therefore, an operational definition may be appropriate. You will still have to defend the definition as the most appropriate for the topic at hand, but only if the negative argues against it. An operational definition simply demonstrates how a policy "operates."

Another way to define a term is to say what it is not, to define by negation. For example, in the illegal-immigration topic, some debaters tried to distinguish illegal immigration from illegal immigrants who later were granted status as refugees. A definition may read as follows: "By illegal immigration we do not mean immigrants who come to America illegally but later are granted refugee status. We mean the bulk of illegal immigrants who come here, not fleeing political tyranny, but seeking American's jobs." Such a definition gives clear ground against which the debate can be judged or the negative can argue. A definition by negation can, of course, be supported by other evidence or definitions. Alone or in conjunction with other definitions, the definition by negation helps give a clear delineation when needed.

A fourth way to define terms is to quote authorities on the subject. Often scholars or commissions set up to study an issue will offer a definition in their books or reports. Often, those definitions are helpful in finding how the term is being used in the public debate on the issue. Furthermore, these "studied" definitions are often more accurate and more helpful than any you can find in a dictionary.

There are many other ways to define terms, but these should give you a good start. When trying to find the best definition to fit your case, think of how a reasonable person with no debate experience would probably define the term. Usually, that is your best hint as to which definition of many to use. It often may be your best defense, as well.

Currently, in the literature about C.E.D.A. debate, there is a controversy over the standard used to judge definitions. Practice, at present, seems to allow the affirmative to get away with any reasonable definition. However, there is a big push now to adopt the *best*-definition standard. In other words, the best definition in the debate is the one that should win. Therefore, affirmatives should be aware that some critics may expect them to have the best definitions in any round. That should be incentive for affirmatives to find the best and most appropriate definitions available.

Criteria for Judgment

Once you have defined the key terms of the resolution, you need to establish the criteria for judging the debate. In order to get started finding a criteria for the case you have chosen, take another look at the evaluative phrase of the resolution. If the phrase says, "is beneficial," ask yourself what is beneficial about the subject. Make sure that you form this benefit in the abstract. You are looking for overall benefits, such as economic, political, or social. For instance, in the nuclear freeze topic, the overall benefit would be political; in this case, world peace and security would be the specific political values. Another source of overall standards are the values outlined by Milton Rokeach (1973). Table 3 lists the terminal values spelled out by Rokeach. Kelley (1981) even suggests that debaters be required to read the works of Rokeach. Rokeach lists abstract values universally held by all people. If any of these values apply, it certainly would qualify for the type of criteria for which most judges look. Not all of Rokeach's list can be used for the purposes of debate, but much of it can. Many critics expect debaters to use these kind of abstract values in non-policy debate. That expectation arises from the idea that values play a big part in non-policy decisions, especially in value decisions.

TABLE 3
Terminal Values

1. A comfortable life	10. Inner Harmony
2. An exciting life	11. Mature love
3. A sense of accomplishment	12. National Security
4. A world at peace	13. Pleasure
5. A world of beauty	14. Salvation
6. Equality	15. Self-respect
7. Family security	16. Social recognition
8. Freedom	17. True friendship
9. Happiness	18. Wisdom

Another possible way to locate a criterion for your case is by perusing works of philosophers, especially political philosophers. Dictionaries or anthologies of philosophy are often helpful to the debate student with little background in philosophy. These can help the student locate certain philosophies more easily than reading original texts. The advantage to using philosophers as support for your criterion is that they often give supporting analysis for use of a certain value or standard. Plato, St. Thomas Aquinas, Thomas Hobbes, John Locke, David Hume, Thomas Jefferson, John Stuart Mill, and Henry David Thoreau are examples of the more predominantly used philosophers in C.E.D.A. debate. A common idea of J. S. Mill, often used in affirmative cases, is that idea that people should be allowed to exercise freedom as long as their actions do not harm others.

More concrete standards are also acceptable in non-policy debate. For instance arguing that having a strong military is good could have served for the standard in the national conscription resolution. Of course, implicit in the more concrete standard are abstract values such as peace and security. By using concrete standards, you are simply putting the emphasis on the more specific. Your criteria contention would simply argue that the team which can demonstrate the best path to a strong military would win the debate.

A final source of criteria are United States' documents, such as the *Constitution*, the *Bill of Rights*, or the *Declaration of Independence*. Encased in these documents are the values and standards on which our society is based. If anything does not match up to these standards, it is fairly easy to call that "thing" detrimental. On the other hand, anything that facilitates American political values would almost assuredly be deemed beneficial. The American political value of the sanctity of human life, as outlined in the *Declaration of Independence*, is often the more supreme of all standards (although there are arguments to the contrary). Anytime you can link your case to the loss or maintenance of human life you are usually on fairly solid argumentative ground. Few things in our culture or political heritage outweigh the value placed on life. Realize in your search for a criterion that it is fine to have more than one criteria if you feel it would be advantageous.

Once you have found the best criterion for your case, the next step is to write a contention supporting that standard as the best standard for judging the resolution at hand. The contention will probably involve two to four sub-points. Table 4 lists an outline of the criterion contention of a case that was written by Cindi Sellinger and Dorise Gray of C.S.U. Chico. (That case is included in appendix "A.") In this example, Cindi and Dorise secured their criterion from the Supreme Court decision of *Shenck v. the United States*.

TABLE 4
Criterion Contention Establishing a Value Hierarchy

Contention I. The criterion for today's round is the Clear and Present Danger Doctrine.

    Sub-point A. First Amendment press freedoms are not absolute.

    Sub-point B. Protection of National Security and human life always outweigh free press and speech.

    Sub-point C. Through application of the Clear and Present Danger Doctrine, the Supreme Court has recognized this hierarchy of life over freedom of the press.

    Sub-point D. Restrictions on media coverage of terrorism are a legitimate application of the Clear and Present Danger Doctrine.

The case argued that restrictions on media coverage of terrorism were justified, the Fall 1985 C.E.D.A. topic. The standard of the Court was to determine whether there exists "a clear and present danger" to U.S. security or to U.S. citizens. If there were such a danger, then restrictions on media coverage would be justified. Also important in outlining the criteria is to try to show that your value is more important than competing values. In other words, you need to establish a **hierarchy of values**. In the first contention of the sample case, that is done in the "B" sub-point that states that national security and human life are more important than press freedom. Additionally, the contention establishes that the first amendment protections of speech and press have never been absolute. A clear and present danger has always provided an exception to the first amendment. Here, a clear hierarchy of life over freedom has been established. Establishing this type of hierarchy is not always necessary. However, some critics feel that such a hierarchy is important in every non-policy affirmative case. In a value topic that asks the affirmative to prove that one thing is more valuable than another, such as the energy and environment topic, it may be important always to establish this hierarchy. In other cases, developing the hierarchy may simply serve as an effective preemption to negative arguments. Every good non-policy debate should come down to a clash on an abstract level, whether or not the affirmative attempts to develop the hierarchy originally. In the debate over restrictions of terrorism coverage, the value clash almost always dealt with life versus freedom. It became easy, therefore, for the affirmative to predict the negative stance and establish the hierarchy in their first speech. As mentioned earlier, political philosophers discussed values, but the focus of their work often established a hierarchy of values. Referring to political philosophers can thus facilitate your argument. Judith A. Best (1980), in her book, *The Mainstream of Western Political Thought*, states:

> The history of political philosophy is in itself evidence that there are a variety of ends or values for man and that these ends or values are frequently in conflict. On the other hand, the history of political philosophy indicates that there is a hierarchy of values. From Socrates, who saw a conflict between two very high things, philosophy and the law, to Nietzsche, who saw conflict between truth and life, each philosopher has ultimately agreed that there is a hierarchy of values. And so, though Socrates taught moderation and attempted to reconcile or mitigate the tension between philosophers and the city, he found philosophy to be higher than the law. So Nietzsche found life to be higher than truth. So Locke and Rousseau declared freedom to be the highest value. So Tocqueville and Aristotle preferred excellence to equality.

> While the philosophers of the Western political tradition have differed in the precise placement of values in a hierarchy, they have agreed that there is and must be a hierarchy. (pp. 13, 14)

Clearly, using a philosopher's arguments can be an effective means to support a particular hierarchy.

Application of the Criteria

After completing the criteria contention, it then becomes necessary to apply that value or standard in the subsequent contention(s). Advocates should argue those contentions or arguments on a more specific level than the criteria contention. For example, say you were debating the desirability of a unilateral freeze on nuclear weapons, and you offer the criterion of world peace. In that case, your contention(s) must show how a unilateral freeze would enhance world peace. To do that, often you need sub-arguments to help persuade on the larger issue. The contentions should set up the big picture, while the sub-points should consist of the figures within that picture. Usually the last sub-point for every contention gives the impact to the contention and the link to the criterion. Table 5 shows an outline of a designative contention on the military-support-to-nondemocratic-nations topic. If you will notice, the first two sub-points do not even discuss U.S. military support or world peace. Those sub-points serve only as sub-arguments to help reach the conclusion found in sub-point "E." That final sub-point also links the criterion of world peace both to military support and to Iraqi expansion, thus serving as a strong conclusion to the contention and strong support for the resolution. Remember, each of these sub-points needs to be supported by at least one piece of credible evidence.

A contention is simply a semi-complete, highly structured argument. It need not prove the resolution true in total, although it may. Often, debaters need to prove a contingent point that would require more space than one sub-point within another contention. In such a case, it is advisable to structure a separate **dependent contention**. For example, the second contention of the sample case in appendix "A" serves as a good example of a dependent contention. That contention simply proves that terrorism threatens the lives of Americans and the national security of this country: the two necessary standards to justify censorship based on the clear and present danger standard (which serves as the criterion for that case). However, the contention does not prove the resolution true *per se*, because it does not show whether media coverage of terrorism presents any particular problem; it merely proves that terrorism is dangerous. The third contention draws the link to media coverage.

TABLE 5
Outline of a Designative Contention

Contention II. Military support to nondemocratic nations deters Iraqi aggression and prevents war.

Sub-point A. Iraq has been expansionary in the past and has a religious doctrine of dominance.

Sub-point B. Iraq is expansionary now.

Sub-point C. U.S. military support can deter Iraq.

Sub-point D. The lack of military support would encourage Iraqi expansion.

Sub-point E. Iraqi expansion almost always involves war; hence, the criterion of world peace is maintained through U.S. military support.

It is also possible to argue what are called **independent contentions**. A case with independent contentions is similar to policy debate's version of the alternative justification case, a strategy that allowed policy affirmatives to win the debate if they won any one of a number of different plans. Often C.E.D.A. debaters will do something similar by presenting two or three independent contentions. In such a case, debaters may need to present the respective number of separate criteria as well. Those criteria are usually outlined in the first couple of sub-points within the contentions themselves, or they can be outlined in the beginning of the case. The advantage to running a case with independent contentions is that, theoretically, you only need to win one contention to win the debate. There is some controversy as to whether independent contentions are valid in C.E.D.A. debate, but many critics accept the concept and many more allow the legitimacy of independent contentions to be argued by the debaters. A note of caution is that you must be sure that your contentions truly are independent. Do not use the same piece of evidence for two separate independent contentions and do not have the concept of one contention depend on a sub-point in another. If either is true, you should reconsider using the independent structure.

DEFENSE OF THE AFFIRMATIVE CASE

When you construct the affirmative case, you need to keep in mind how you plan on defending the case for the remainder of the debate. The second affirmative constructive speaker must be able to refute the negative attacks from 1NC and rebuild the affirmative case. In order to do that 2AC will need evidence to support the exact same sub-points in 1AC. Therefore, when preparing the affirmative case, debaters should simultaneously prepare 2AC. Often, debaters may want to set up the negative by planting a weaker argument in 1AC, and, in 2AC, read much stronger evidence to make the negative argument look foolish in retrospect. Be careful using any kind of strategy, though. C.E.D.A. has tried to avoid the game playing that could so easily plague the activity. Strategy can backfire, as well. In the illustration just given, a few critics expect the 1AC to contain the best arguments for a given position. Putting the weaker argument first may incite those few critics to look unfavorably toward your position. However, for the most part, as long as there is not a major shift in your argumentation, such a strategy will most often, for most critics, help your position.

What is clearly necessary, though, is for 2AC to have at least one piece of evidence for every sub-point in 1AC. In other words, you are really writing 1AC twice, just with different evidence. Try to use as many different sources as possible too. The reason that you need so much evidence in 2AC is because of the preponderance of evidence standard borrowed from the law courts for debate purposes. Preponderance of evidence merely says that the weight of evidence on a particular issue has a bearing on who wins that issue. Numbers of evidence cards can sometimes influence the "weight" of argumentation. If the affirmative reads five pieces of credible evidence from separate sources on a particular sub-point and the negative none, the affirmative will almost always win that point on preponderance of evidence alone. Therefore, it is important for 2AC to be able to read evidence to rebuild the affirmative case.

The second affirmative should always begin his or her refutation by briefly restating the original point from 1AC. This should be done by indicating which 1AC contention and sub-point you are extending. For instance, 2AC should say something such as, "In terms of our original argument in contention one, sub-point 'A', where we said that human life is the highest value, the negative said . . . " After reminding the audience of your original argument, then use four-point refutation for the rest of the argument. The addition of restating an original argument transforms four-point refutation into **five-point rebuttal style**. (Four-point refutation will be discussed at length in the next chapter.) Second affirmative should do the same thing for every single sub-point on case, even where the negative missed a sub-point. In that case, 2AC should simply note that the affirmative is winning that point due to negative drops. 2AC should also tell the critic why that dropped argument is important to the debate.

The job of 2AC is twofold, however. Not only must 2AC rebuild its own case, but it must also refute negative attacks. 2AC must remember to do both refuting and rebuilding. A common error made by novice debaters is that they frequently do one but not the other. A rule of thumb to follow is to argue one sub-point at a time and refute the negative attacks first, and then rebuild with new evidence last. Often re-explaining 1AC evidence can be an effective way of refuting negative attacks. Then when reading further documentation, you will make your argument look even stronger. You must be sure to "extend" your 1AC arguments. In other words, do not simply repeat the case argument, but give some new insights or new analysis as to why the affirmative position is best.

SUMMARY

In this chapter we have looked at ways to research and analyze a debate topic, techniques for writing an affirmative case, and hints on how to defend your case in 2AC. There are many ways to analyze and do research, but hopefully the suggestions offered here will be helpful in getting started. With regard to writing the case, this chapter outlined methods to define terms, establish criteria, and apply criteria. Finally, debaters need to give the second affirmative speech some forethought before the debate begins. Following the steps outlined in this chapter can help the novice debater approach his or her first debate round with a little more ease and perhaps expertise. Truthfully, debate is a difficult activity to understand from a book, manual, or lecture. This manual can only hope to give you the background you need to get started. Much of what you learn will be through trial and error and by doing. After watching your first debate and especially after experiencing your first debate, much of this will become much more clear. While this chapter has discussed how the affirmative can write its case, the next chapter will outline the negative approach to non-policy debate. The fourth chapter will also discuss some additional ideas about negative as well as affirmative approaches to non-policy debate. And chapters five and six will cover sound vs. fallacious reasoning.

3 | NEGATIVE

NEGATIVE BURDENS

In debating against the affirmative, the negative's minimal burden is simply to disprove the affirmative case. Technically, the negative need not prove or establish anything. Remember, the affirmative has the **burden of proof**, which means that the affirmative debaters have to prove the resolution true. The negative debaters, on the other hand, have no resolution to uphold and thus have a wider range of argumentative options open to them. Their minimal burden is merely to disprove the affirmative stand.

There are numerous methods that the negative may use to disprove the affirmative. The negative can resort to negative philosophies, *prima-facie* arguments, definitional arguments, topicality challenges, point-by-point refutation, and value objections. Some of these approaches are necessary and some of them are optional. What is important to remember is that the more you prepare and practice, the more proficient you will become. Debating on the negative side has some unique difficulties. For instance, you rarely know what the specific affirmative arguments are until the debate begins. That's why preparation is so important. This chapter will address these approaches and difficulties in order to help you handle each of the negative speaker positions.

THE NEGATIVE AND PRESUMPTION

While the affirmative has the burden of proof, the negative enjoys what is called **presumption**. There are two basic types of presumption: natural and artificial. **Natural presumption** is the notion that we "presume" things will remain as they are until good and sufficient reasons are found to change them. This applies to beliefs and values as well as policies. Presumption is non-evaluative. It does not say that the present system or our present values are good; it merely says that our values and policies will remain until reasons to change are found. While natural presumption deals with things as they are in reality, artificial presumption exists to provide rules for a contest or controversy. **Artificial presumption** establishes agreed upon rules, such as the "innocent until proven guilty" standard of our courts. In debate the rule is that "one who asserts must prove." Because the affirmative has asserted that the resolution is true, they therefore must prove that assertion. In this case, the negative enjoys presumption simply because the affirmative has made an assertion; the negative has made none. Brydon (1986) argues that artificial presumption is the best paradigm to use in non-policy debate. Scott and Wynn (1981) write, "For consistency, for parsimony, and for clarity, we suggest that presumption should be against the resolution" (p. 26). Since the negative is thought to have both natural and artificial presumption, if the debate comes down to a tie, the negative will win. More importantly, presumption puts the debate into perspective. As a negative debater, you realize that the affirmative has to prove certain things. If the affirmative does not prove all of the stock issues or all of the causal links, then the affirmative cannot win. The negative can "press" the affirmative for these links and stock issues during the round; if the affirmative cannot clear up the flaws in their argumentation, then they will lose the debate, even if the negative does nothing else but press for proof. Of course, there are exceptions to this rule, as there are to any rule; however, most critics will vote for the negative if the affirmative cannot answer a negative press for proof on a crucial issue. It is not advisable for a negative team to do nothing but press. A negative will lose most of their rounds if that is all they do. Being able to press the affirmative for crucial information is merely suggestive of the advantage the negative has because it enjoys presumption. The negative still has the **burden of refutation**, which means that the negative has to provide support for any assertion that they make. In other words, once the affirmative presents a *prima facie* case (one that has all the stock issues and necessary information), the negative debaters need adequate arguments backed up with credible sources if they hope to win the debate. The affirmative, however, has the burden of proof; hence the negative has a slight advantage with presumption on their side.

Typically, negatives in non-policy debate divide up responsibility between the first and the second negative constructive. First negative usually deals with "on case," or point-by-point refutation of the affirmative case. Second negative usually offers the negative case, called "off case" or value objections. The rest of this chapter addresses each of these constructive speeches and their respective approaches.

FIRST NEGATIVE--REFUTING THE DEFINITIVE STOCK ISSUE

The first negative constructive (1NC) speaker usually attacks the substance of the affirmative case. There are exceptions to this which will be discussed later. For now, it is important to explain what a typical first negative should argue.

The Negative Philosophy

The first words out of the 1NC speaker's mouth should be the **negative philosophy**. A negative philosophy consists of the negative value for the debate at hand. Table 6 lists the outline of a sample negative philosophy on the media and terrorism topic. The reason for establishing the negative position immediately upon speaking is because the first negative speaker must be perceived as standing on his or her own constructive ground. Were 1NC to begin with a refutation of the affirmative case, he or she would be perceived as being on the defensive. Rarely do debaters win a round when they merely argue against their opponents. Debaters need to build their own case and position as well. Additionally, this negative philosophy can serve as a "theme" to be carried through the rest of the debate. Negative debaters should attempt to prove that the negative philosophy is the superior value.

TABLE 6
Sample Negative Philosophy

The negative philosophy for today's round is that freedom of the press is a superior value.

Sub-point A.   Freedom of the press is an important value of our society.

Sub-point B.   The first amendment protections including protections on press have a heavy presumption against abridgment.

    1.   The loss of a handful of lives, although tragic, is not justification for jeopardizing the freedoms for which our founding fathers died.

    2.   The highest value is that of freedom over life.   Patrick Henry stated it best, when he said, "Give me liberty or give me death."

Sub-point C.   The only time that press can be restricted is when the national security of the United States is threatened directly, not when a few hostages' lives are at stake.

Recall that the affirmative is trying to establish a value hierarchy or at least a value position. A good non-policy debate should come down to a "clash" of values. As an example, affirmatives on the media coverage of terrorism topic would argue that the press should be restricted to save hostages' lives. Their criterion was the sanctity of human life. Negatives, on the other hand, offered the negative philosophy of the first amendment freedom of the press. Much of their argumentation from then on would be trying to prove that press freedoms are more important than protecting the handful of people who may die from media mistakes during hostage crises. They might argue that our forefather's died so that the press could be free, and therefore our society values a free press over human life. Additionally, the negative might argue that the only valid restriction of the press is to preserve the national security of the United States in a time of war, not merely when a group of hostages are in jeopardy. Having such a negative philosophy is extremely helpful in establishing an arguable position.

The negative philosophy in 1NC should take up no more than 30 seconds to 1 minute introducing the negative value to be defended. Negatives should have two or three negative philosophies from which to choose, depending on the affirmative case they hit. The negative philosophy should simply state what the value position of the negative is and why it should be superior to the affirmative value position. The argument ought to be structured the same as any original argument in debate, i.e. in outline form. Notice that the philosophy outlined in Table 6 is a fairly short argument. Only a couple of the sub-points will require evidence. The negative philosophy is both a statement of position and an argument. During case refutation, the negative philosophy should be mentioned to help demonstrate the superiority of the negative value. In other words, 1NC refutation ought to provide a clash on the concrete as well as on the abstract (value/philosophical) level. It is extremely important for the negative to argue this type of value hierarchy. Furthermore, the negative philosophy ought to be explored even more fully in the "off case" arguments of the second negative constructive speech.

Prima-Facie Argumentation

After offering the negative philosophy for the round, the 1NC speaker should then consider whether the affirmative case is ***prima facie***. *Prima facie* literally means "at first look." In simpler terms, the affirmative needs to have satisfactorily fulfilled all of the stock issues for non-policy debate or they are not *prima facie*. Technically, if the affirmative fails to fulfill even one of the stock issues or any other major issue, they should lose the debate.

If the first negative constructive speaker concludes that either of the two non-policy stock issues are missing from the affirmative case, he or she can then issue a *prima-facie* challenge. To do that, all 1NC needs to do is demonstrate to the critic that this necessary component is missing from the affirmative case. A common mistake made by beginning non-policy debaters is to leave out a criterion, which, of course, is part of the definitive stock issue. Most critics are fairly compassionate with novice debaters, and most will not give a loss to a team on *prima-facie* grounds alone. That does not mean that negatives should not issue *prima-facie* arguments. Once you make the challenge, if the affirmative cannot adequately explain the absence of a criterion, their position will be weakened considerably, and they will more than likely lose the debate. If, on the other hand, the affirmative is able to come up with some kind of criterion when pressed for it, at least their credibility will be hurt. Moreover, the challenge, which caused the affirmative to come up with a criterion, will also make it easier for the negative to clash with the affirmative value position.

On quasi-policy topics, often lack of affirmative solvency becomes a *prima-facie* issue. On the unilateral-nuclear-freeze topic, negatives pressed for proof that the world would follow the U.S.' lead. If the world did not, nuclear problems would not only persist, but worsen. The negative, therefore, would win the debate.

Definitional Arguments

Often affirmatives will choose tricky definitions that that attempt to sidestep negative argumentation. Unfortunately, sometimes the implications of these "tricky" definitions do not become apparent until the end of the debate when it is too late to argue them. At that point the negative will have probably lost the debate due to lack of foresight. To avoid this problem, it is important to take issue with any definition that seems suspect of being non-standard. One definition to be wary of is one that lacks support from sources. As you will remember from chapter two, the most common form of definition in non-policy debate is the dictionary definition. While 1AC is speaking, be sure to listen closely for definitions that lack support from a dictionary or an expert. If you hear an unsupported definition, you will need to do two things in refutation. Note to the critic that the affirmative definition lacks support and provide a substantiated definition (*eg*. dictionary).

Another common non-standard definition used by affirmatives is a narrow definition. Often affirmatives will extract a single word or phrase from an unabridged dictionary. When you hear an extremely short or narrow definition, you may want to take issue with it. Again, you need to note first that the definition is narrow. However, narrowness is not in itself bad, so you also need to give a reason why the narrow definition is unreasonable. Second, you need to provide a longer, more general definition. Ideally, you will have the same source on file that the affirmative used and can clearly demonstrate the nature of the context of the affirmative's definition. If not, a more complete definition from any source will do.

Other unreasonable definitions may include definitions which are too broad or take the word out of context of the resolution. What is important to understand from this discussion is that if you hear a questionable definition, you need to take issue with it. First, suggest why it may be unreasonable and, second, offer an alternative definition. If you fail to do either of these things, most critics will allow the affirmative definition to stand. Failing to show why the affirmative definition is unreasonable gives the critic no reason to accept your definition over theirs. Additionally, failing to offer an alternative definition leaves only one definition for that term in the debate, the affirmative's. While the affirmative definition may be inappropriate, it is the only one, and it will stand. Most critics feel that something is better than nothing.

C.E.D.A. predominantly uses the reasonable-definition standard discussed thus far. However, another standard seems to be gaining popularity, the best-definition standard. When using this standard, the negative speaker need not prove that the affirmative definition is unreasonable, but he or she merely has to prove that the negative's definition is better than the affirmative's. In order to prove that your definition is best, you can do a number of things. First, you may argue that your definition better takes into consideration the historical context of the resolution. Second, you can argue that, in the context of the resolution *per se*, your definition makes more sense. Third, you may even argue that your definition allows for more clash between affirmative and negative and hence is best for debate purposes.

Both the "best" and "reasonable" standards have been accepted in debate practice. Unfortunately, it is difficult to tell which, if either, a critic accepts. Unless you know a critic's preference, use the one with which you feel most comfortable. Be cautioned, though, many critics do not accept the best-definition standard. Nevertheless, whichever standard you use, be sure to issue any definitional arguments in 1NC. Many debate judges see definitional arguments as operational issues that must be addressed in the first speech; 2NC is too late.

Topicality arguments

While examining definitions, the 1NC speaker may note that the affirmative is not topical due to a misused or unreasonable definition. Recall that topicality arguments question whether the affirmative case is within the bounds of the resolution. For example, on the religious activism topic, the affirmative was required to prove that religious activism in politics harmed the American political process. Some affirmatives ran cases which argued that religious groups told their followers how to vote. The harm was that large numbers of puppet voters put the political process in the hands of a few fundamentalist religious leaders. Many negatives, however, questioned whether telling people how to vote was actually "activism in politics." Consequently, a topicality argument grew out of a definitional concern with that phrase. If this were the case, the negative would have to word the complaint in the form of a structured topicality argument. Were the negative to win that argument and prove to the critic that telling people how to vote was not "activism in politics," then technically the negative ought to win the debate on the topicality argument alone. Jan Vasilius (1980) argues, "In value debate . . . the affirmative case stands as the sole interpretation of the resolution. It is, therefore, not a partial issue. If the negative succeeds in winning topicality there is a total victory" (p. 53). Table 7 gives an example of how the activism topicality argument might be phrased. Notice how the argument is arranged: first, standards or definitions; second, violations of those standards; and, third, impact of the violations. There are two different ways to argue topicality: one, you can use the affirmative's definition against them; or, two, you can argue that the affirmative's definition is unreasonable and suggest an alternative. Table 7 looks at the first way of arguing.

TABLE 7
Sample Topicality Argument

The affirmative case is not topical by the affirmative's own standards.

Sub-point A **Standards.** The affirmative defines *activism* as political activism by people who go beyond normal citizenship to try to change existing political norms.

Sub-point B **Violations.** The affirmative violates their own definition on two levels.

1. Voting. The affirmative argues that religious groups tell their followers how to vote, yet they define activism as "going beyond normal citizenship." To the extent that voting is not beyond normal citizenship, the affirmative is non-topical by their own definition.

2. Telling people how to vote is not quite political activism. Telling people how to vote is religious propaganda, with dubious political implications. After all, how do we know whether these people vote as they are told?

Sub-point C **Impact.** The affirmative is non-topical on two counts. Unless they resolve this discrepancy, they should lose the round.

Regardless of the approach taken, topicality arguments are an effective way to argue in academic debate. As a negative debater, you should always ask yourself whether the affirmative case is on the topic or not. If there is any question whatsoever, you should consider running a topicality argument. Many critics expect topicality arguments to be run in 1NC. The reason is that they feel definitional issues such as topicality are operational issues that should be resolved as early in the debate as possible. Second negative constructive may not get away with running a topicality argument. If you are debating team debate, you need to be aware of this requirement.

Often, topicality arguments are difficult to think of while preparing the 1NC speech. Often, novice teams will finish with a debate and say to themselves, "we should have run a topicality argument; that case was clearly non-topical." To avoid resorting to such hindsight, make a conscious effort to consider topicality before every first negative presentation.

Argue Criteria

When arguing criteria, there are at least four approaches that you can take. The first approach consists of the *prima-facie* requirement discussed earlier. This approach can only be used if the affirmative lacks a criterion. The second approach is to accept the criterion, but to show that the affirmative team does not uphold it. For example, on the military-support-to-non-democratic-nations topic, some affirmatives gave the criterion of preventing an aggressor's expansion. One way to argue that criterion would be to accept it as the standard for judgment, but to show that U.S. military support does not prevent such expansion. You could argue that non-democratic countries change leaders regardless of support and that various leaders choose for themselves which alliances, if any, they will form. When using this technique of arguing criteria, negatives could have used the historical example of the Samoza regime in Nicaragua. The U.S. supported him for years, but he was overthrown in spite of U.S. aid (or because of it). Until recently, the Soviets had significant influence in Nicaragua, and we had little. If the negative debaters could prove, in Nicaragua and overall, that U.S. military aid does not prevent aggressive expansion, they could win the debate.

A third approach to arguing criteria is to demonstrate the flaws of the criterion itself. For example, an argument against the criterion of the sample affirmative case in appendix "A" was that the clear-and-present-danger standard only applies in time of war, not during terrorist activities. Of course, the second affirmative had evidence demonstrating that terrorism is analogous to war; however, the negative could still win this argument through effective extensions in its rebuttal presentations. Demonstrating that the criterion is flawed is a good first step toward winning a debate.

The fourth approach is to argue that your negative philosophy is superior to the affirmative's criterion. The sample negative philosophy at the beginning of this section represents the beginning stages of such an approach. All you need to do is to establish the hierarchy of your value over the affirmative's. In the example given, the negative attempts to show that the freedom of the press is a more important value, in this particular case, than the sanctity of human life.

The latter three approaches to arguing criteria are not mutually exclusive. You could feasibly argue that the affirmative criterion is flawed, that it is inferior, and "even if" it is not flawed or inferior, it does not apply anyway. When you use this type of "even if" argument, be sure that the critic and your opponents understand that it is a conditional argument. In other words, when you argue that the criterion does not apply, that does not mean that you forfeit your arguments that it is flawed or that the negative philosophy is superior. Simply make your intentions clear to the critic and your opponents.

FIRST NEGATIVE--REFUTING THE DESIGNATIVE STOCK ISSUE

After giving the negative philosophy, examining the *prima facie* nature of the affirmative case, contending with definitions, issuing topicality arguments, and arguing criteria, the 1NC speaker then needs to argue against the designative contention(s). In order to do this, the negative speaker ought to use point-by-point refutation. The most common form of this type of refutation is called **four-point refutation**. Four-point refutation asks the debaters to use the following four steps: first, to briefly restate the opponent's argument; second, to briefly introduce your argument; third, to give evidence or analysis; and, fourth, to offer an impact or summary statement. Using this style, 1NC needs to argue the heading of each contention, the logic of each contention, and/or every sub-point of each contention. Do not skip any sub-points. Argue each sub-point in the order that it was presented by the affirmative. Most importantly, when restating your opponent's argument, be sure to state the substructure of their case. You will actually say things like, "in terms of contention I, sub-point "B," where the affirmative argues . . . " If you need to save time, often it is fine to *group* arguments. For instance, if there are two sub-points in a contention that are similar, you may be able to refute both of them at the same time. Be careful not to group dissimilar sub-points; a good team will quickly point out that you left one of their arguments unanswered, even though you made it appear as though you argued it.

Four-point refutation can be mastered quickly with a fair amount of practice. Table 8 gives an example of four-point refutation. This type of refutation provides a formula approach to answering arguments. As mentioned the formula starts with the first of four steps, which is to **briefly state your opponent's argument** that you are refuting. That means a number of things. One thing it means is that you should only *briefly* state the argument. Do not help your opponents by completely arguing their argument over again. Simply repeat their claim statement. The reason you do this is to tell the critic and your opponents exactly which argument you are refuting so that they can keep an accurate record of it on their flow-sheets. Another thing that this means is that you need to state the letter or number of the sub-point each time you move to the next of your opponent's arguments. Failure to do the latter may muddle the debate. Additionally, if the critic does not know which sub-point you are arguing, he or she may not be able to record your arguments, which could affect whether you win or lose the round. Throughout the debate you need always to state clearly which sub-point you are arguing. This is not merely a requirement of first negative, but it is a requirement of every debater throughout a debate.

The second step of four-point refutation is to **briefly state the claim statement for your argument**. A common mistake frequently made by novice debaters is that they forget this step, but it is very important. Often, novice participants will read evidence card after evidence card, without ever giving an introductory claim statement for that evidence. One reason for having claim statements is so that those recording your speech can write down the claim statement and then listen to the evidence. If you fail to introduce your evidence or analysis, often those listening will not understand what you are trying to get out of it. The third step is to **give the evidence or analysis** to support your claim. When reading evidence, be sure to give full source citations. In C.E.D.A., most critics expect at minimum the following: name of expert, the credentials of the expert, the title of the book or document, and the full date of the citation. Be prepared to defend the credibility of the sources you use. The final step of four-point refutation is to **give the impact to your argument**. Impact statements are brief summary statements of the evidence or analysis. These statements usually indicate why you think you should win a particular argument.

In the example in Table 8 notice the use of full source citation, the reference to affirmative case substructure, and the brevity of steps 1, 2, and 4. Emulation of this style will help you win numerous debates. However, a formula is not all that you need, you also need to be able to formulate lines of argument.

TABLE 8
Example of Four Point Refutation

1. They said in Contention II, Sub-point A, that religious groups will enact federal legislation to suit their own whims.

2. We say that the federal courts would strike down any religiously inspired legislation.

3. Documentation for this comes from J. Phillip Wogeman, professor of Christian Social Ethics at Wesley Theological Seminary, in *The American Academy of Political and Social Science Annals,* November, 1979. Wogeman says, "And religious groups, when they go lobbying for (their own theological views) must expect them to be struck down eventually by the courts even if they are enacted into law."

4. The impact to this evidence is that our government has checks and balances, such as the courts, to prevent a single interest from dominating the legislative process.

LINES OF ARGUMENT

Deny Proof

Your best argument against a point is to show that the point has not yet been proven. Occasionally, affirmatives will issue a claim statement for an argument, then read evidence which does not even come close to supporting that claim. This happens more frequently in novice division. Your first response, then, in refuting that claim is simply to point out exactly what the evidence did say. To do that, simply quote the crucial part of the evidence to jog the critic's mind. Then mention the claim statement to reveal the discrepancy. In order to become good at this type of analysis, you need to listen carefully to evidence while it is being read by the other team.

Directly Deny the Argument

Another argument against a point is to directly deny the truth of it. For instance, if the affirmative argued that Iraq is expansionary, a good argument would be to directly deny it and read evidence that gave some analysis as to why Iraq is not expansionary. However, direct denial is not always possible. What if Iraq is expansionary? What do you do then? Well, life has not ended. One thing that you will learn in debate is that there is an argument against everything.

Weaken Arguments

If you cannot directly deny an argument, you can bring in facts that help weaken the argument. Perhaps a good argument against Iraq being expansionary is that it does not have the economic means to be expansionary. In other words, maybe it is expansionary in theory, but in practice, it has not the means. The war against Iran and the economic embargo has drained Iraq of its economic means to expand elsewhere. While Iraq may want to expand, currently it cannot.

Turn-Around Arguments

Another option is to argue a **turn-around**, which is defined as taking what seemed to be an opponent's argument and using it to support your position. Some common arguments used during the military support topic should give you an idea of how to approach first negative constructive. Affirmatives would argue that the Soviets were by nature expansionistic. Negatives responded, however, by turning around that argument. They argued that merely believing that the Soviets were expansionary was problematic and gave rise to an unnecessarily aggressive U.S. foreign policy. The nature of U.S. foreign policy had caused the Soviets to be extremely defensive. An outgrowth of their defensiveness was that they were more expansionary than they would have been otherwise simply because the U.S. tried to involve itself in every part of the world that the Soviets had an interest. The Soviets feared being forced out of the resource picture by the aggressive U.S., so they used military solutions to protect their interests. So what had been an affirmative argument (U.S. military support to other countries was necessary to prevent Soviet expansion) became a negative argument (the Soviets were forced to appear expansionary due to an aggressive and misguided U.S. foreign policy).

Question the Recency of Evidence

There are other things that you can argue in 1NC, as well. One is to argue the recency of the evidence. Recency of evidence is always important in debate. Depending on the argument, if the evidence is not recent (for example, not within the last five years), it may be of questionable validity. An effective way to argue against outdated evidence is to point out how outdated it is and then read evidence that postdates it. Of course, you need to explain why postdated evidence is better. One possible justification for postdating opponent's evidence is because the issue under scrutiny has changed radically in the last few years; what was once true of that issue is true no longer. For instance, say your opponent reads a 1976 piece of evidence indicating that most states have shoddy drunk driving laws. You can point out that drunk driving legislation has changed drastically since then due to the activities of groups like Mothers Against Drunk Driving (M.A.D.D.). Therefore, your opponent's evidence clearly is outdated.

Question Authority

Another thing that you can do is question the authority of the evidence. If the authority is a person, be sure his or her credentials are related to the claim. For example, on the nuclear freeze topic, affirmatives often quoted Hans Bethe, a Nobel prize winning physicist, who advocated a unilateral freeze. Although apparently a credible source, his credentials (physicist) were not related to the claim (foreign policy). Besides relevance to the claim, also look for whether the source of evidence is biased. On the United Nations topic, many teams quoted the Heritage Foundation, a conservative political organization. Opponents quickly took issue with that source, due to its conservative bias. Of course, not all information from biased sources should be discarded; however, it is a point of contention that should be raised. While relevance to claim and bias are important elements of source credibility, sometimes opponents will not qualify a source at all. If questions in cross examination do not establish a source's credibility, then you can indict the source on the grounds that he or she could be the janitor at the *New York Times* for all you know. Furthermore, you should argue that the unqualified evidence should be discounted in the debate.

Question Opponent's Logic

While the source is important to scrutinize, so is the logic of your opponent's argumentation. Often, novice debaters will attempt to prove a general claim statement with only one example. For instance, the third contention of the sample case in appendix "A" uses example reasoning to prove that the media are feckless. For each of their sub-points, they give an example to prove a general statement. A negative speaker, in this case, should question whether the affirmative is using correct example reasoning. Example reasoning is a form of argument that moves from specific instances to a more general claim. Two of the tests for example reasoning are to ask whether sufficient examples have been provided and to ask whether those examples are typical. If either of these tests are violated the affirmative is guilty of a **hasty generalization**. A first negative speaker can simply argue that one example is not sufficient and challenge the affirmative to come up with more examples. Another option is to read evidence that documents counter examples. The reason for providing counter examples is because a third test for example reasoning is to be able to account for negative instances. If the affirmative cannot do that, the negative will probably win the argument. Example reasoning is only one type of logic to be questioned. Chapter five of this text outlines the tests for sign, analogy, causal, *etc.* Use them.

Point Out Contradictions

Another logical problem affirmatives may have involves contradictions, especially when 1AC attempts independent contentions. Debate resolutions concern complex issues. Often an affirmative case, when trying to deal with those complexities, accidentally contradicts itself. The first negative ought to point out those apparent contradictions and ask the affirmative speakers to resolve them. In addition, ask the critic to discount both sides of the affirmative contradiction until it is resolved.

Argue Lack of Impact

Another logical flaw often included in an affirmative case is the lack of an impact. 1AC may argue that something is true, but gives no reason why we should care. If there is no reason to care or no impact, first negative ought to mention that. For example, someone may argue that thousands of people commit computer fraud every year. The question left unanswered by that statement is whether computer fraud is good or bad. First negative could simply say, "They argue computer fraud. I say, so what? There is no impact given by the affirmative as to whether computer fraud is good or bad. The argument is therefore irrelevant."

Argue That 1AC and Darwin Have Much in Common: No Links

Another logical flaw commonly committed in debate is faulty cause-to-effect reasoning. Therefore, the first negative speaker should always look for weak causal links in the affirmative presentation. Be especially wary of a case that argues that the world will end if we act or believe a certain way. Often, such drastic argumentation includes a faulty causal link somewhere. You simply need to point out where the weak links are and offer some possible alternative explanations. For example, on the nuclear freeze topic, debaters tried to argue that unless we freeze now, there will be a nuclear war within five years. The first negative speaker should simply offer some other plausible interpretations of the future. For instance, you could argue that new technology, such as the strategic defense initiative, will actually prevent nuclear war. You could also suggest that lack of a freeze will make people even more scared to use the advanced weapons of the future.

Press for Information

Finally, you can simply press the affirmative for any requirements you feel they have not met. For example, if you feel that there is no impact to an argument, ask them to provide it. A negative press is usually worded thus: "The affirmative needs to provide some impact to this argument. Without impact the argument is worthless." All of these approaches to first negative are valid. By no means is the information presented here all inclusive, however.

There are many other approaches that a first negative speaker can take. These are merely suggestive of the ways 1NC can refute the affirmative case. Table 9 includes a list of possible claim statements that you can use when employing the second step of four-point refutation. The claims were written by Thompson (1971). Notice that the statements here are in very simple language. All you need to do in using four-point refutation is simply issue the arguments clearly so that your critic and opponents can understand what you are saying.

SECOND NEGATIVE CONSTRUCTIVE SPEECH

The second negative constructive (2NC) speech in non-policy debate usually develops the negative case, completely separate from the arguments presented up until that time in the debate. 1NC arguments are referred to as "on-case" or "case-side" arguments. 2NC arguments are referred to as "off case" or "value objections (V.O.'s)." A common mistake made by novice debaters is that they fail to take full advantage of 2NC. It is really a waste of time for 2NC to spend time on case, so that usually should be avoided.

TABLE 9
Possible 1NC Claims

This argument is an isolated example.
This argument is a false analogy.
This is faulty cause-to-effect reasoning.
This is a nice theory, but let's look at the facts.
Actually the reverse is true.
This is true, but . . .
The facts are true, but the inference is wrong.
The underlying assumption is faulty.
In another place Mr. (Ms.)_____says the opposite.
This is true, but it is a benefit and not a harm.
This is not significant.
The opposition has never quantified the extent of the harm.
My opponent left out some details in citing this example.
The statement is true, but let's go one step further.

(pp. 199-200)

Yet, many novices do not know what to do in second negative. Value objections, as currently practiced in C.E.D.A., are general attacks on the values implied by the affirmative case. More and more critics are requiring that value objections apply to the affirmative case. General attacks upon the resolution usually do not have much affect, unless they can be linked to case side. The best way to approach 2NC from the perspective of a novice competitor is to look at the resolution and develop a few sound arguments against it. Look at the underlying values implied in refutation of the resolution. Remember, that when you use these general arguments in a debate you are going to have to link them somehow to the affirmative cases that you hit, but that is not so difficult. The key, again, is to look for values. On the U.N.-membership-is-no-longer-beneficial topic, 2NC's had a significant amount of success running value objections that talked about the value of world cooperation. Affirmatives were asked to show that the U.N. was no longer beneficial to the U.S., implying that the worth of the U.N. should be determined by each nation separately. Negatives objected to that value of nationalism and offered value objections supporting a world government. All second negative had to do in order to link that V.O. to the affirmative case was to simply find a place in the affirmative argumentation that supported the concept of nationalism.

Ideally, however, once the beginning debater has had some experience debating in intercollegiate competition, he or she can begin to compile a list of opposing affirmative cases. With that list, he or she can develop specific value objections for each of the different types of cases. C.E.D.A., more and more, is beginning to require on-point value objections. The general ones, even when linked to case, are seen as weaker arguments, than the more directly responsive ones.

Value objections (V.O.'s) are delivered in outline form in the same manner as the affirmative case. (See the sample value objection in appendix "B.") You need to do a number of things in each V.O. A suggested method of structuring V.O.'s is to include 4 steps: introduction, link to the affirmative case, implications of affirmative value, and the impact of those implications. Table 10 lists the outline of a sample value objection which employs this structure.

TABLE 10
An Outline of a Value Objection

I. We object to the affirmative value of supporting dictatorships with U. S. Military Support.

  A. (Introduction of negative value.) The negative advocates the value of sanctions for dictatorships.

  B. (Link to affirmative case.) The affirmative supports the value of giving military aid to dictatorships, as they indicate in Contention II sub-point A, of 1AC.

  C. (Implications of the affirmative value.) The support of repressive regimes is bad.

    1. Dictatorships use U.S. aid to subjugate their people.

    2. Common people from these countries hate the U.S.

    3. Marxist influence grows in a country that resents the U.S.

  D. (Impact.) If Marxists are successful, the U.S. may never have influence over that country again, and such a victory for communism may threaten the post-cold-war, democratic resurgence.

When you are writing the value argument, make the "A" sub-point of the V.O. the introduction of your value. In the "B" sub-point, try to find a specific sub-point on case to which you can link the value objection. For instance, if the case talks about giving military aid to El Salvador and other right-wing dictatorships, you can link a dictatorship V.O. to that type of case. Therefore, in the "B" sub-point of that V.O., you would state something to the effect that "the affirmative supports the value of giving military aid to right wing dictatorships as they indicate in Contention II, sub-point A of 1AC." Sub-point "C" of the value objection "objects" to the value of giving military aid to dictatorships. Arguments may include the fact that dictatorships use U.S. military support to subjugate their people. Other arguments may try to show that, because the U.S. supports dictatorships, citizens from those countries hate the U.S. Another argument may try to prove that Marxist revolutionaries become more influential in a dictatorship supported by the U.S. After developing the argument, the fourth step in a value objection is to give an impact statement.

In the example given above, a possible impact statement would be that if the Marxists are successful, the U.S. may never have influence over that country again. That type of impact statement would be especially effective if the affirmative criterion were maintenance of U.S. relations with all dictatorships in order to prevent Marxist influence.

In summary, V.O.'s should be linked to case, should develop analysis through sub-points, and should give impact. The format offered here is only suggestive. Experiment with various formats to see what works best for you. Some non-policy topics are easier than others for developing off-case arguments. The best place to start looking for ideas is the resolution itself. Just be sure to make the best of the second negative. It can often make the difference in a debate round. Also, be sure to work closely with your partner, so that your value objections do not contradict the arguments from first negative constructive.

SPLIT-CASE RESPONSIBILITIES

First and second negative occasionally may want to share the refutation of the affirmative case. Say 1AC includes two contentions. The negative team may decide that 1NC should refute *contention I* and 2NC should refute *contention II*. Some critics dislike this approach because they feel that it puts an unfair burden on the first-affirmative-rebuttal speaker, and they feel that first negative has the responsibility to refute the entire case. In debate, *silence* often means *consent*, and failure to refute all of 1AC is no exception for some critics.

However, sharing the refutation of the affirmative case seems to be gaining acceptance by many critics as a legitimate negative approach. It does offer some advantages. First, it can save valuable preparation time. Each team in a debate has a limited amount of preparation time allotted to them (normally, five or six minutes each). If you use all of your allotted time preparing for an early speech, you will have none later. Having little or no preparation time left can be devastating, especially for novices. Because affirmative arguments are rarely known until presented, novice debaters often use much or all of their preparation time for 1NC, Obviously, the first negative speaker will not need to use as much preparation time if he or she does not have to prepare for the *entire* affirmative case. The second negative speaker may then prepare to refute the remainder of 1AC while the debate transpires.

Sharing case refutation also allows the first negative speaker to be more communicative. With fewer arguments to refute, 1NC will be able to speak more slowly and concentrate more effectively on delivery and quality of argument. Additionally, if the first affirmative speech is extremely lengthy (due to fast talking or *spread* debating), split refutation may also be advantageous to allow the negative team the speaking time necessary to refute *all* affirmative arguments. Finally, split refutation allows second negative the opportunity to focus on a particular 1AC argument, which the negative team may find difficult to understand or difficult to refute (due to lack of negative evidence). Additional time may be necessary simply to think of an appropriate response or to locate necessary evidence.

Split refutation does not necessarily preclude second negative from issuing value objections. In fact, it shouldn't. 1NC should cover approximately three-quarters of the affirmative case, thus leaving ample time for 2NC to issue one or two key value objections and to cover the remainder of case easily.

SUMMARY

In this chapter, we discussed the standard approaches to first and second negative as practiced currently in intercollegiate non-policy debate. First negative usually refutes the affirmative case, and second negative objects to the values implicit in that case. Occasionally, however, the negative may deviate from the norm to split the responsibilities of refutation. The next chapter will address additional alternatives to the traditional first and second negative, as well as look at some other issues in non-policy debate.

4 | ADDITIONAL PRINCIPLES

REBUTTALS IN NON-POLICY DEBATE

A good way to develop your rebuttal style is to watch and emulate a practiced rebuttal speaker. Perhaps your teacher or coach can arrange for you to see a practice debate between senior members of your school's forensics team. As you watch, note the concise use of words and the sound organization of the speech. Also, note the way in which entire sets of arguments are synthesized.

One of the more difficult aspects of debate to master is the art of rebuttal speaking. Novice competitors tend to make one extremely common mistake: They simply repeat constructive arguments. However, repetition bores all audiences and wins few debate ballots. In rebuttals, speakers must *extend* arguments. In other words, the rebuttal speakers need to give some new analysis as to why they think they are winning the argument at hand. You need to answer the question: Why am I winning this point? The answer to that question can come in any number of ways.

Strength of Evidence

First, you can simply point out to the critic reasons that your evidence use is superior to your opponents'. Remember, your argument should involve new analysis. If you have already explained that your evidence is superior, then saying so again is fine, but it is not an extension. One type of evidence extension is simply to claim preponderance of evidence. Recall that preponderance of evidence means that the strength of your evidence outweighs the value of your opponents' evidence. Showing that you have read far more evidence on a point is one way to claim preponderance of evidence. In affirmative rebuttals especially, where the negative had read no evidence against your case, you can claim that you win a certain argument on the preponderance of evidence standard alone. Say for instance that you have read four pieces of evidence throughout the debate on a certain point; your opponents have read none. That is a time to claim preponderance of evidence.

Another related extension is to compare the credibility of your sources with the credibility of your opponents' sources. On a certain point, if you have read evidence from a law professor, a U.S. Senator, and the Attorney General of the U.S., and your opponent has read evidence from a local politician, you can claim that your sources are more credible; hence, you should win the argument.

Comparison of Arguments

Besides showing that your evidence use is superior, you may also reveal holes in your opponents' arguments, while showing the strength of yours. Notice that in both the examples given thus far, there is an implied comparison. A good rebuttal will show both the weakness of an opponent's argument and the strength of yours. A poor rebuttal will only address one side of the controversy. Thompson (1971) quotes a debater's rebuttal which is both showing the holes in his opponent's argument, while building his own:

Finally, our opponent claimed that removing covert activities would destroy the capacity of the CIA as an information-gathering agency. Three answers: First, already 80% of the CIA's information comes from public sources. Second, most of the remaining information is obtainable without using clandestine means. Third, satellites and other technological devices are constantly being perfected as information-gathering agencies. (pp. 199-200)

In this excerpt, notice how the debater made an implicit comparison between his opponent's argument and his own argument. The debater destroyed his opponent's argument by building the idea that information is and can be obtained without the CIA. Notice also how succinct his arguments are. Such word economy is important for a good rebuttal because ordinarily you only have four minutes to answer all arguments. Were his opponents to speak again, they would need to do the same thing: show the holes in his argument and build their own. Usually, it is good to begin with demonstrating opponents' weakness. If you were to refute the above argument, think first about how to show a weakness in his logic. The biggest hole in his argument is that alternative means cannot account for 100 percent of CIA information-gathering. That would be your first response. Next, you would have to rebuild your argument that the CIA would lose its information-gathering function were it to abandon clandestine means. Through the use of evidence, you would have to show that there is some CIA clandestine activities that bring valuable information, and that there is no substitute for those activities. In your first response you revealed the hole in your opponent's arguments; in the second you have rebuilt your original argument.

Burden of Rebuttal

By doing that, you have shifted the burden of rebuttal back to your opponent. You see, the burden of rebuttal shifts back and forth between affirmative and negative alternately in a debate. The one with the burden of rebuttal at the end of the debate loses. All you have to remember is both to show the weakness in your opponents' arguments and to show the strength in yours. You also need to give an extension to, rather than a repetition of, your original arguments. In the above example, many novices would simply have responded by repeating that without clandestine means, the CIA would lose its information-gathering function. Such repetition, as stated earlier, is not an effective method of arguing because it does not involve an extension to the argument. Additionally, you would still be stuck with the burden of rebuttal, were you to merely repeat an argument.

New Arguments

The final rule of rebuttal of which you need to be aware is that you cannot issue a *new* argument in a rebuttal speech. That means that you cannot begin an entirely new line of argument; however, you can read new evidence and give new analysis on an old line of argument. For instance, in the example given above, the argument that there is information that the CIA needs that can only be obtained through clandestine means is not a new line of argument. It is merely new evidence and new analysis extending the argument that the CIA would lose its information-gathering function without clandestine activities. However, a new line of argument might entail arguing that the Air Force would not be able to operate effectively without CIA information. This is a new argument and not an extension of the old argument about losing information.

Responsibilities of Rebuttal Speakers

Each rebuttal speaker in non-policy debate has a different responsibility. The first negative rebuttal (1NR) speaker argues against the case extensions of 2AC. Since 2NC speaks immediately before 1NR, due to the negative block, 1NR need not deal with off-case arguments at all. The first affirmative rebuttal (1AR) speaker is the first speaker to argue both on case and off case. 1AR must address the entire negative block, usually 12 minutes, in a four-minute speech. Consequently, he or she must use time as effectively as possible. A rule of thumb to follow is to spend about two-and-a-half minutes arguing against second negative's off-case arguments and about one-and-a-half minutes against 1NR. Second negative rebuttal and second affirmative rebuttal must follow the same format as 1AR. Table 11 demonstrates the formats to follow in rebuttals. The last three speeches, as you will notice, are the most difficult because they deal with both on case and off case.

TABLE 11
Rebuttal Coverage

First Negative Rebuttal	On-Case Only
First Affirmative Rebuttal	On-Case and Off-Case
Second Negative Rebuttal	On-Case and Off-Case
Second Affirmative Rebuttal	On-Case and Off-Case

THE PRESUMPTION-SHIFT AFFIRMATIVE CASE

Often non-policy resolutions are worded so that the affirmative seems to have presumption. For example, the illegal-immigration topic suggested that the affirmative prove illegal immigration detrimental. One could easily make a case that you "presume" illegality to be detrimental, and therefore the affirmative should enjoy presumption on that topic. Some affirmative teams have attempted to run just such a presumption shift in the first affirmative constructive. While it seems that the affirmative could easily be afforded this option, many critics feel that presumption should always rest with the negative. This discrepancy has caused Scott and Wynn (1981) to state, "The place of presumption in (non-policy) debate, at present, is not well defined" (p. 25). The purpose of this discussion is twofold: first, it is important that affirmatives know how to run a presumption shift if they feel one applies; second, negatives need to know how to refute a presumption shift if they come against one.

Affirmatives who want to argue a presumption shift ought to realize that most critics feel presumption should always rest with the negative. Arguing a presumption shift would only be fruitless in front of those critics. Furthermore, the only time that presumption comes into play is when the debate is a tie; the team with presumption at the end of a tied debate will win.

While the predominant view in C.E.D.A. is that presumption lies with the negative, that does not preclude the affirmative from attempting to claim presumption. Some critics will consider those arguments. Richard Whately, a 19th century argumentation scholar, was the first to borrow presumption from the legal arena and apply it to argumentation theory. Whately (1963) suggests in his book, *The Elements of Rhetoric*, that a single argument from probability can cause presumption to shift from one advocate to another. A suggested paradigm for C.E.D.A. is that it be assumed that the negative has presumption unless the affirmative wants to argue for it. That is why an affirmative claiming presumption is called a presumption shift: The affirmative is attempting to shift to their advantage something that traditionally belongs to the negative.

In order to claim presumption, the affirmative merely needs to give an argument as to why they feel presumption rest with the resolution. The earlier discussion of the illegal immigration topic gives a good illustration of how one might approach such argumentation. Sproule (1976) and Zeuschner and Hill (1981) suggest that Whately had in mind a psychological presumption that rests in the mind of the audience. Brydon (1986) rightfully rejects that approach as unreasonable for academic debate. However, one can believe that presumption can shift without necessarily accepting the concept of psychological presumption. Brydon himself admits that the wording of C.E.D.A. topics has afforded the affirmative presumption on some topics. If that is that case, then critics should allow advocates to argue presumption if they should choose to do so.

Once the affirmative makes some arguments to claim presumption, they should then offer the impacts to the shift. The obvious impact is that in case of a tie the affirmative would win. Another impact is that now that the affirmative has presumption, the negative now has the burden to disprove the resolution. If the negative fails to provide *prima-facie* argumentation, then, technically, they should lose on *prima-facie* grounds. Of course, few critics would accept this added negative burden. Nevertheless, the debaters should be allowed to argue the issue.

Once the negative is faced with a presumption shift, they can do one of two things. First, they can argue that they actually have presumption. They should always make the argument that presumption should always rest with the negative and that the affirmative has no business trying to shift what belongs to the negative. The affirmative has asserted that the resolution is true and has the burden to prove that assertion. You will win the approval of most critics with that statement. You can also try to win back presumption by showing that the affirmative's rationale for taking it in the first place is wrong.

A second thing that the negative can do is to take the affirmative's challenge and actually offer a negative case. Most negative's would jump at the chance at pulling out all of their general negative arguments and running them in 1NC. In other words, the negative grants the affirmative presumption and takes on the burden of proof. In that case, the negative needs to present a *prima facie* case, with the definitive and designative stock issues. Negative advocates, facing a presumption shift, need to act as though they are the affirmative, but they should also refute the affirmative case, just to be safe.

NONVERBAL COMMUNICATION

An often overlooked variable is the effect of a debater's nonverbal behavior on the outcome of a debate. The importance of a confident, professional demeanor cannot be overstated. In team debate especially, your nonverbal reactions to your partner's arguments can have a dramatic effect on a critic's interpretation of the debate round. A beginning debater occasionally will be embarrassed by a partner's line of argument, for instance. Common responses to such embarrassing comments may include one or more of the following behaviors: slouching in the chair, hands over your eyes, rolling your eyes, feigning to cough, looking away, looking disgusted. groaning, putting your head down on the desk, tossing an evidence card in the air, shrugging your shoulders, laughing *etc*. While all these behaviors may seem extreme and even humorous, they really do occur. The end result of such nonverbal behavior can only be deleterious. Instead of negative nonverbal reactions, at least remain calm and expressionless. However, the best response is for you to be confident and composed. And more often than not, your partner's argument isn't as bad as it may sound. Remember, sometimes it's the unusual and unique argument that wins the round. Realize, too, you also may make an argument or give an answer that you don't really like. Be calm and confident, and give the best answer you can. Don't allow yourself to look troubled or trapped. Let the judges decide whether your team's answer was bad. You don't have to decide it for them.

CROSS EXAMINATION

One of the unique contributions by C.E.D.A. to academic debate was the development of the cross examination format. After each constructive during a debate, the constructive speaker must be cross examined by a member of the opposing team. There are no written rules concerning which speaker of the opposing team must question the previous speaker. However, the most common method is for the speaker who *does not speak next* to do the questioning. For example, once first affirmative constructive speakers finish their presentations, the second negative speaker usually questions them. The first negative speaker, who speaks next, then may use the cross examination period to listen to the cross examination and/or prepare for 1NC. The logic behind this method is that the next speaker will have more preparation time. In the typical debate, second negative questions first affirmative, first affirmative questions first negative, first negative questions second affirmative, and second affirmative questions second negative. See Table 12. Notice that each speaker both asks and answers questions once each.

Most tournament and classroom formats limit the cross examination period to three minutes. During that time, the questioner and the respondent attempt to accomplish a number of goals. The questioner's goals include clarifying points, setting up future arguments, and exposing opposition weaknesses. The respondent's goals include answering questions in a knowledgeable fashion, avoiding possible traps, and gaining control of the questioning period. While attempting to fulfill these objectives, the questioner and respondent face the audience, not each other. Cross examination is as much for the benefit of the audience as for the debaters.

TABLE 12
Typical Cross Examination Format

Constructive	Respondent	Questioner
First Affirmative	First Affirmative	Second Negative
First Negative	First Negative	First Affirmative
Second Affirmative	Second Affirmative	First Negative
Second Negative	Second Negative	Second Affirmative

The Questioner

When you are the questioner, the first order of business must be to clarify any points of which you are unclear. Failure to clear up cloudy areas will usually result in problems later in the debate. Simply ask direct, **open questions**, such as, "What is the thesis of your case?" or "Explain the essence of the "A" sub-point on contention one." Ask these questions with the tone of voice of already knowing the answer, as if you are probing for a flaw in their case. Avoid appearing confused or overwhelmed.

Additionally, as questioner you may want to set up future arguments. In order to do that, try to pin your opponents to a position. For instance, on the overemphasis-of-the-press topic, negative questioners attempted to set up future value objections about the harms of press restrictions. Questioners would attempt to lead the affirmative to admit that, if the press has been emphasized, then the press must be restricted. A question/answer session may proceed as follows:

Negative:	"Do you agree that the American judicial system has given a lot of power to the press?"
Affirmative:	"Yes, in fact they overemphasized it."
Negative:	"Do you think this emphasis is harmful?"
Affirmative:	"Of course it is harmful. Our D sub-point shows you that."
Negative:	"As a society, then, what are we going to do about it? Should we fix it?"
Affirmative:	"Yes, we should fix it, but that's beyond the scope of the resolution we are debating today."
Negative:	"So we should fix it? Right?"
Affirmative:	"I said, 'yes.' But that's beyond the scope of the topic."

Negative:	"If we can show you that anything less than the present level of emphasis would destroy democracy, how would that be non-topical?"
Affirmative:	"You can't show that. I don't know. It's beyond the scope. We don't have to show solvency. This is a factual topic."
Negative:	"Where do you argue that this is a factual topic?"
Affirmative:	"It's obvious. We don't need to argue that."

Notice some things here. First, the questioner asks **closed** (or yes/no) **questions**. Except when clarifying points, ask closed questions whenever possible. Second, the questioner asks a series of yes/no questions. This allows you to set up the premise of the argument (in this case that the press has been emphasized). Later, you establish the logical conclusion from the premise. Were you to start with the conclusion (that we need to solve for press emphasis), you may not have done as well. Notice that the earlier questions are easier for the respondent to answer. Always start with the less threatening questions to establish the premise. Third, notice that the questioner maintains a position less than *overemphasis*. The Spring 1988 C.E.D.A. topic reads, "Resolved: That the American judicial system has *overemphasized* freedom of the press." By maintaining a position of "emphasis" or "a lot of power," the questioner avoids granting the debate to the affirmative. Fourth, the questioner follows up on arguments made by the respondent. For example, the respondent tries to argue that this is a factual topic. However, the questioner realizes that the respondent did not argue that, so the questioner asks for the supporting data from the case, knowing that none exists. Finally, the respondent admits that something should be done about the harm from an unrestricted press. The questioner wants that admission, because that will set up the future value objection. When second negative issues the value objection on the harms from a restricted press, he or she can remind the audience and critics that the affirmative admitted that we should "fix" the problem.

Pointing out the flaws in the other's position serves as a third purpose for the questioner. There are many potential flaws that can be exploited. The lack of a threshold (*eg.* failure to show when we cross the threshold from emphasis to overemphasis), the lack of harm, the lack of strong evidence, the commission of fallacies, or the failure to establish a causal link all consist of possible flaws to be explored. Remember, as a questioner you must always phrase your ideas in the form of a question. Avoid making statements or speeches. Making statements usually causes your opponent to argue with you. The entire cross examination then may become a shooting match. Also, avoid being argumentative or rude. Simply ask questions the way you would ask a friend. If the respondent becomes angry or rude, try to maintain your poise. If your questioning fails to move forward as planned, do not force the issue; simply, start another line of questioning.

Most importantly, be sure to maintain control. In other words, do not allow the respondent to ask you a question (except to clarify a question you asked). If the respondent asks you a question, kindly say, "This is my cross examination, please answer *my* question." Also, avoid allowing the respondent to talk beyond a reasonable amount of time. If the respondent begins to speak too long, simply say, "thank you, that's fine." If he or she continues to speak, say the same thing a couple of additional times progressively more forcefully until you receive compliance. Sometimes, appealing to fairness can also be helpful. While they still are talking, say, "I only have a short time, and I'd really like to ask a number of other questions," or "You still have another speech to say all of this; let me use my questioning time now please." Again, avoid becoming frustrated or rude.

There are a few things that you can do to make your questioning easier. First, before the debate begins, you can prepare a list of generic questions on both sides of the topic. If all else fails, at least you will have something to say during your three minutes. Second, while the other team is delivering a constructive speech, be sure to jot down some possible questions that you may wish to ask. Third, as your first question, ask an open question, such as, "Could you explain your criteria to me?" While the respondent answers, you will have time to get your thoughts together.

The Respondent

The most important objectives for the respondent are to know the issues surrounding the topic and to know your arguments and evidence for the particular debate. Knowledge of the topic is important for all aspects of debating, but especially for the role of respondent. The questioner can ask you any question on the topic. The more you read about the topic, the better a debater you will be and the better you will handle cross examination. Of particular importance is for you to know your affirmative case if you are an affirmative respondent or to know your negative arguments if you are a negative respondent. For instance, a questioner may ask you about the methodology of a particular study you cite. Ideally, you should be able to answer that question without looking at your notes. If you do not know the answer, try to avoid having your partner prompt you or shuffling through books or evidence not yet read in the debate. It may hurt your credibility. If you do not know the answer, simply try to answer as best you can using information from your previous arguments. Simply admitting that you do not know the answer to a question is also an option. Such an admission probably will not lose you the debate, but answering a question incorrectly could get you into trouble. Suggest confidently that you could clear up the issue later in the debate if it became important. The best options are to study the topic and memorize your arguments, so that you can answer all questions accurately and to your advantage.

A second goal for the respondent is to avoid getting trapped. There are a number of things you can do. First of all, before the debate, discuss with your partner potential traps that you want to avoid. Decide the safest position to take, and be ready to argue that position later. Second, during the cross examination, avoid being pinned down to a dubious position. For instance, the questioner may ask, "If we prove that the Iraqis are warmongers, we should win the debate? Right?" Avoid answering such questions "yes." Instead, just say "no," or say something like, "First of all the Iraqis are not warmongers, and, even if you could prove that, you would not necessarily win the debate." Third, destroy the premise of the question before answering the question. In doing so, use specific evidence from your speech. For instance, in the example given above, you might say, "The Iraqis are not warmongers; I proved that with my response on contention one, 'B,' the Jones evidence, that showed that Kuwait had been waging an economic and covert war with Iraq. Iraq's invasion was totally justified." The more specific you can be in citing your evidence, the better.

Finally, avoid answering tricky yes/no questions with a simple *yes* or *no*. Give your explanation first. Otherwise, your opponent may not allow you to give an explanation at all, and you will appear rude trying to give one. For instance, a questioner may ask, "Have the Iraqis been involved in any military action in the past twenty years?" Obviously, the answer to that question is yes, but a simple *yes* answer will allow your questioner to build a premise to a line of questioning that may get you into trouble. You should answer, "Any aggressive action by the Iraqis is purely defensive and protective; I read you that evidence in my last speech. So yes, they have been involved in military action, but they are not expansionistic." In a sense, you are predicting where the line of questioning is headed and trying to stop it before it bears fruit.

While being knowledgeable and avoiding traps are important for the respondent, important also is trying to take control of cross examination if possible. One way to do that is to continue answering as long as your questioner allows you to speak. Simply keep talking and summarizing evidence and points that you have made earlier in the debate. However, when the questioner does stop you, be polite and let him or her pose the next question. Another thing you can do is ask a question of your questioner. If he or she answers, you have just taken control of the questioning period. Continue asking questions politely until your opponent discovers the error or the cross examination ends. Additionally, if your opponent makes a statement, rather than asks a question, attempt to converse with him or her. A conversation is much less of a threat than if the questioning were to continue. However, avoid getting into an argument with your opponent. A conversation is one thing; an argument is a completely different issue.

As the respondent, try to remain poised and calm. Do not ever act frustrated or as though your opponent's question has upset you. There will always be a question or two that will baffle you. Try to use arguments that you have already made in order to compensate for what you may not know, but be honest. Lying can only get you into trouble. Furthermore, understand debate theory and use it when answering questions. For instance, it is helpful, at times, to point out to affirmative questioners that it is they, not you, who have the burden of proof. Additionally, know all of the answers to generic questions on the topic. Whether debating in an argumentation class or on the intercollegiate circuit, a number of questions usually become standard. Know and rehearse answers to those questions. Finally, whether you are the questioner or the respondent, feel free to use humor when appropriate. Being facetious, for instance, can be a way out of a difficult situation. C.E.D.A. has attempted to make debate audience-centered. Humor is one way to help accomplish that goal, and cross examinations are the most likely place to incorporate a funny line or two.

EMORY SWITCH

Reportedly, the technique known as the Emory switch was developed originally by some debaters from Emory University. The way in which C.E.D.A. debaters have incorporated the format is to *switch* the responsibilities of first negative and second negative. In other words, first negative, rather than refute the entire affirmative case, offers value objections instead. And second negative, rather than offer value objections, refutes the affirmative case instead.

The benefits to the negative are obvious. The most blatant benefit is that the negative team has much longer to evaluate the affirmative presentation. If the affirmative case is difficult to understand, sometimes resorting to an Emory switch is the only viable defense. The Emory switch also enables the negative to offer a greater sophistication of argument earlier in the debate. When debating a complex topic, often the negative position is not sufficiently developed until second negative. Offering off-case arguments in 1NC allows the negative platform to be constructed early. Second negative is then able to cross-apply the well-developed value objections onto the affirmative case. Failure to use this strategy on a complex topic occasionally results in a wasted first negative constructive. Finally, an Emory switch forces first affirmative rebuttal to assume what are normally time-consuming, second affirmative responsibilities. 1AR has barely one-quarter of the time usually used by 2AC: thus, granting the negative a significant time advantage.

Many critics dislike the Emory switch for the very reason that it is unfair to 1AR. However, if the affirmative team uses the Emory switch to put pressure on 2NC, that disadvantage can be minimized. To do this, second affirmative constructive must refute the value objections in the same manner as normally done in 1AR: by grouping arguments and economizing word use. With the remaining five to six minutes, 2AC can go back on case to extend it with more evidence. You see, while the second negative speaker prepares to refute case, he or she normally assumes that 2AC solely will refute 1NC value objections. When the second affirmative speaker extends case with more and different evidence, however, many second negatives will be unable to refute the additional case material without dropping arguments. First affirmative rebuttal, then, becomes manageable, because it can refer to additional 2AC arguments and to the subsequent negative drops. Second affirmative might also consider issuing an **add-on contention**. If time allows, search through your affirmative file and throw a few pieces of evidence into an additional designative contention. Read that contention during the last minute or so of 2AC. Add-on contentions are a completely legitimate strategy, which are not necessarily restricted to a defense against an Emory switch. However, if you call the add-on contention a *2AC underview*, it is usually more palatable for the critic.

As a negative team, it is normally unwise to use the Emory switch all of the time. On the intercollegiate circuit, you will be perceived as a weak team that uses the strategy simply to prepare for 1AC. Use the technique only when necessary or strategic to do so. Additionally, when using the Emory switch be sure to address all operational issues in 1NC. That means that first negative still needs to offer topicality arguments, definitional arguments, criteria arguments, and *prima facie* arguments. Be cautioned; some critics and instructors do not accept an Emory switch. When in doubt, pose the question to your critic or instructor before the debate.

PREPARATION TIME

Most debate formats allow a limited amount of preparation time between speeches: usually 5 minutes total for each team. The team which speaks next is charged with prep-time use. For instance, if 2AC uses one minute of preparation time, the affirmative team will have four minutes left. Critics will usually announce the amount of prep-time remaining; however, just to be sure, you should ask them to do so.

Affirmative Preparation Time

Most affirmative teams attempt to save the bulk of their preparation time for the first affirmative rebuttal. The reason for this is obvious. 1AR has to answer twelve to thirteen minutes of negative argumentation in one-third of the time. Additionally, second affirmative constructives should already be prepared for their presentations, and second affirmative rebuttal is not as crucial as 1AR. Ideally, with a five-minute preparation rule, 2AC should not need more than a minute of preparation time. Remember, 2AC has three minutes of cross-examination time after 1NC in order to prepare. 1AR requires at least three minutes, and, if possible, save approximately one minute for second affirmative rebuttal. Table 13 lists the suggested prep-time use for affirmative as well as negative teams.

Negative Preparation Time

Normally, first negative constructive requires much of the negative's preparation time: approximately three minutes in a debate with a five-minute preparation rule. Most often, 1NC does not know what the affirmative case entails, so it's only obvious that the first negative speaker will need more time. Second negative constructive and first negative rebuttal should not require any prep time at all. Most of 2NC's arguments are prepared prior to the debate. And any value objections developed during the debate can be done so during other speakers' cross examination or preparation time. 1NR needs no prep time because it can be prepared during 2NC. The first negative speaker should know the context of 2NC's arguments, so there should be no need to listen. That time can be used instead to prepare for the next speech. 1NR should be ready to speak by the end of 2NC however. At times, opposing questioners may prematurely end the questioning of 2NC if 1NR is still preparing during the cross examination. The final two minutes of negative preparation time then can be used for second negative rebuttal.

TABLE 13
Suggested Use of Preparation-Time
Based on a Five-Minute Limit per Team

Next Speaker	Aff. Time Used	Neg. Time Used
First Affirmative Constr.	Not applicable	
First Negative Constr.		Three minutes
Second Affirmative Constr.	One minute	
Second Negative Constr.		Zero minutes
First Negative Reb.		Zero minutes
First Affirmative Reb.	Three minutes	
Second Negative Reb.		Two minutes
Second Affirmative Reb.	One minute	
Total	**Five minutes**	**Five minutes**

Further Suggestions for Using Preparation Time

Most critics prefer that you do not use all of your preparation time if you don't really need to. Also, a team is perceived as better prepared which has prep time left at the end of the debate round. Occasionally, however, the opposite occurs, and a team runs out of preparation time early in the debate. A speaker then may have to speak without having adequate time to prepare. Fortunately, there are some things you can do to mitigate the effects of such a tragedy. First, during the course of the debate, think of things you'll want to say during your rebuttal. Write those ideas on the far right side of your flow-sheet: that way, at the end of the debate, at least you will have something to say.

Second, practice taking an adequate flow-sheet, so that you can speak easily from it. If you do not have time to write out your responses, you will be able to read earlier arguments with ease. Thus, you can refute opponent's arguments and extend yours without having to write out everything. Truthfully, even with judicious use of preparation time, you will probably never be able to write out all of your responses anyway. Through trial and error, debate forces you to learn the skill of thinking while you speak. Taking a good flow-sheet is the first step toward developing that skill.

Finally, what you do before the debate can also help you deal with lack of preparation time. Sit down with your partner and write out some stock responses for each of the rebuttals, especially 1AR. Write the arguments on index cards and keep them with your evidence. Also, the more you prepare and practice the less you will need to use prep time. Know your arguments, as well, so that you can summarize them without really having read your flow-sheet. And, make sure that your evidence file and brief folder are in order, so that you don't have to waste time looking for that one perfect piece of evidence.

COUNTERWARRANTS

Counterwarrants are general resolutional attacks by the negative. Rather than link arguments to the affirmative position, the negative instead refutes various examples of or warrants for the resolution. The negative usually justifies counterwarrants by demonstrating that the affirmative interpretation of the resolution is in some way unreasonable or narrow. For instance, say the resolution asks the affirmative to prove that the U.S. military is unprepared for a conventional war. The affirmative case, rather than arguing something significant, argues, instead, that soldiers' boots are fitted too tightly and are constructed very poorly. In such an instance, the negative could reasonably argue that the design of combat boots is an insignificant example on a topic filled with tanks and missiles. When arguing that the affirmative has interpreted the resolution narrowly, you are arguing that the affirmative is guilty of a hasty generalization. As discussed earlier, a hasty generalization is committed when the affirmative violates the tests for example reasoning.

When setting up a counterwarrant as a negative advocate, you ought to prove the hasty-generalization argument first. In order to do that, simply argue standards, violations, and impacts, just as you do in a topicality argument. The standards are that the affirmative must discuss the whole resolution (nicknamed "whole res" on the intercollegiate circuit). In other words, the examples the affirmative chooses must be significant and pervade all aspects of the resolution. Another standard involves meeting the tests for example reasoning. In this case, the violations are that the affirmative advocates are not "whole res," because they are discussing combat boots, an insignificant aspect of the topic. That example also violates the standards for example reasoning. The example of combat boots neither constitutes a sufficient number of examples, nor is it a typical example.   The impacts then are twofold: First, the affirmative advocates must lose because their case is insignificant; second, counterwarrants are justified because the affirmative case is too narrow. In other words, the critic cannot get an accurate picture of the resolution if all four debaters discuss only combat boots.

If the negative team wins the hasty generalization argument, then any general negative arguments should be allowed to stand. On the conventional-military topic, the negative would not be constrained to discuss only combat boots, but could discuss some of the significant aspects of the topic. For instance, you could argue that our fighters, bombers, and helicopters are of sufficient strength to support ground troops in any war. As a negative advocate, remember that it is always best to directly refute the affirmative case. Counterwarrants should be a last resort, and always should be run as an addition to case refutation. Furthermore, a hasty-generalization argument is an operational issue and should be argued in first negative constructive. However, many teams argue counterwarrants as a general rule, with no justification. Some critics seem to be accepting this approach. Regardless of which approach you take, however, do not make your counterwarrant(s) your only argument.

When affirmatives are faced with counterwarrants, they should deny the justification for counterwarrants, as well as refute the content of the arguments. If a hasty generalization is argued, refute standards, violations, and impacts if possible. Try to answer all arguments. On the example given above, for instance, try to justify the significance of your topic. Although the poor design of combat boots is a dubious position to take when measuring conventional military strength, there are arguments that you could make supporting the significance of it. You could argue that ground troops are the most important measure of conventional strength. You could argue further that studies (if there are any) demonstrate that poor footwear on combat troops results in significant fatigue early in battle. And, finally, perhaps you could even argue that tired soldiers lose battles. If the critic accepts your case as significant, the counterwarrants should not carry as much weight in the decision.

LINCOLN/DOUGLAS DEBATING

Lincoln/Douglas debating requires an advocate to research, write, and defend an affirmative case. Chapter 2 covers those affirmative requirements. The L/D debater on the negative side of the proposition must refute case and offer value objections. Chapter 3 discusses that information. Basically, there are only a few notable exceptions to team debate of which the L/D participant must be aware.

First, the time constraints and speaking order differ from team debate. Table 1, on page 2, demonstrates those differences. Note that the affirmative participant speaks three times, and, in order to compensate for that, the negative constructive is much longer than the affirmative's. Second, the negative speaker, having only one constructive, must refute case *and* offer value objections in a single, twelve-minute constructive. If you are the negative debater, you should spend about six to eight minutes refuting 1AC and around four to six minutes offering off-case value objections. A third difference is that the affirmative only has six minutes in 1AR to refute value objections and extend the affirmative case. You do not have a second constructive in which to properly extend case. It will be impossible to read one piece of evidence for every point in 1AC. Therefore, in preparing to be an affirmative L/D participant, you need to carefully select the points you want to extend and diligently choose the evidence to do so. Finally, realize that you do not have the benefit of using your partner's cross examination time in which to prepare for your speech. Therefore, you need to have your briefs and evidence extremely well organized.

SUMMARY

This chapter covered some additional issues involved in non-policy debating, such as rebuttal speaking, counter-values, and presumption shifts. The key to good rebuttals is to extend arguments. The key to running presumption shifts is to determine whether the resolution is worded in such a way as to give the affirmative presumption. If it does, then it behooves you to manipulate that to your advantage. You really have nothing to lose in arguing for a presumption shift as long as you do not make the presumption shift your only argument. Finally, the key to running a counter-value, again, depends upon the topic. If the topic is a quasi-policy topic, a counter-value may apply. Also discussed were strategies for handling cross examination, Emory shifts, and preparation time. While some of the ideas contained in this chapter may be a bit advanced, they are nevertheless important for the debater who wants to truly understand the activity.

5 | USING SOUND REASONING

Debaters must be able to use sound reasoning. Failing to do so can harm any chances of winning a debate. Conversely, debate helps an advocate develop critical-thinking skills. While the ability to think critically may seem like an innate quality, actually, it is something that can be learned. And debate enhances learning.

DEDUCTIVE AND INDUCTIVE REASONING

An understanding of **deductive and inductive reasoning** can help develop your ability to reason effectively and to debate more easily. Some logicians feel that all argument is basically deductive, and some say that all argument is basically inductive. However true either of these positions may be, making a distinction between these two types of reasoning can help an advocate develop sound arguments.

Many texts in the communication discipline define induction as specific to general arguments and define deduction as general to specific arguments. However, these definitions are incomplete at best and inaccurate at worst. Ray and Zavos explain,

[I]n deduction the conclusion is required by the premises, or reasons, whereas in induction it is not. In other words, in deduction the conclusion states no more than what is stated in the reasons taken together; in induction the conclusion goes beyond what is stated in the reasons.

The definitions often given for deduction and induction make the two processes parallel and exactly opposite: deduction is defined as reasoning from general statements to particular statements, and induction is defined as reasoning from particular statements to general statements. These definitions are inadequate. For one thing, it is clearly possible to reason from general statements to other general statements: for example: "All periods of high employment are followed by periods of inflation, all periods of inflation are followed by periods of high unemployment; thus, all periods of high employment are followed by periods of high unemployment." It is also possible to reason deductively from particular to particular; for example: "A is taller than B, B is taller than C; thus, A is taller than C." It is also argued by some that many inductions involve reasoning from particular statements to other particular statements.

Deductive Reasoning

Deductive reasoning is often described as any argument that develops from a general premise to a specific conclusion. That definition is inadequate as explained above; a more accurate definition is one offered by Howard Kahane, in his book, *Logic and Contemporary Rhetoric*: "if its premises are true, then its conclusion must be true." An example of a deductive argument is the following **categorical syllogism:**

Major Premise:	All U.S. presidents have been men.
Minor Premise:	Abraham Lincoln was a U.S. president.
Conclusion:	Abraham Lincoln was a man.

The first two sentences in this argument are the two premises. The first sentence is the **major premise**, the second sentence is **the minor premise**. Notice that as of the publication date of this book, both of the premises are true. Therefore, the **conclusion of the syllogism**, the last sentence, must also be true. Of course, in order to be sound, the syllogism must have **validity** as well as **truth**. The following formula must be applied to all syllogisms: **Truth + Validity = Soundness.**

The standard of truth is met if the premises are true. Truth of the premises is often checked by applying the principles of inductive argument. (That will be discussed later.) The standard of validity is met if a few simple procedures are followed. For a categorical syllogism, such as the one above, those principles are simple. First, the syllogism must follow the following format:

Major Premise:	All A's are B's.
Minor Premise:	C is an A.
Conclusion:	C is a B.

Major Premise:	All A's [middle term] are B's [major term].
Minor Premise:	C [minor term] is an A [middle term].
Conclusion:	C [minor term] is a B [major term].

In addition to this format, the categorical syllogism may only introduce three items. If it introduces a fourth term, it is invalid. The following categorical syllogism is therefore invalid because it does not follow the above formula:

All men are mortal.
Socrates was *mortal*.
Therefore, Socrates was a *man*.

Note that the middle term, *man*, is not in the middle. In order to be valid, though, the middle term needs to be distributed at least once. This argument is invalid because it does not follow the *ab-ca-cb* format outlined above. Logically, just because Socrates is mortal does not force the conclusion that Socrates is a man. As far as the syllogism is concerned, Socrates could be something else that is mortal, such as a dog or a tree. Realize that validity and truth are completely separate concerns. In this case, for instance, the syllogism is true (we know that Socrates was indeed a man), but invalid.

With truth and validity as the two tests for a syllogism, there are then four possible outcomes when evaluating a syllogism. They are as follows: first, true and valid; second, true but invalid; third, valid but untrue; and finally, untrue and invalid. The following four syllogisms represent an example of each:

True and Valid:

Major Premise:	All men are mortal.
Minor Premise:	Socrates was a man.
Conclusion:	Socrates was mortal.

(This syllogism is true because the major and minor premise are true. It is valid because it follows the *ab-ca-cb* format outlined above.)

True but Invalid:

Major Premise:	All men are mortal
Minor Premise:	Socrates was *mortal.*
Conclusion:	Socrates was a *man.*

(This syllogism is true because each sentence is true. The syllogism is invalid because the term, *man*, in the conclusion should switch places with the term, *mortal*, in the minor premise.)

Valid but Untrue:

Major Premise:	All fish are blue.
Minor Premise:	The U.S. president is a fish.
Conclusion:	The U.S. president is blue.

(This type of syllogism is the source of stereotyping and prejudice. This syllogism is valid because it follows the format outlined above. It is untrue because fish come in a variety of colors, and the U.S. president, at last look, was not a fish.)

Untrue and Invalid:

Major Premise:	All fish are green
Minor Premise:	Our university president is green.
Conclusion:	Our university president is a fish.

(The syllogism is untrue because fish come in a variety of colors, and university presidents have many qualities, but *green-ness* is not one of them. This syllogism is invalid because the term, *fish*, in the conclusion should switch places with the term, *green*, in the minor premise. Notice that even if the major premise (all fish are green) were true, there are more green things in the world than fish. Therefore, just because the president is green does not guarantee that he/she is a fish.

Another sound categorical syllogism is one in which the major term is negated (in the minor premise) and the middle term also is negated (in the conclusion). The syllogism, to be valid, must follow the following format:

Major Premise:	All A's are B's.
Minor Premise:	C is not a B.
Conclusion:	C is not an A.

Here obviously the middle term is not distributed; however, the categorical syllogism of negation is an exception to that rule. The following example illustrates a true and valid syllogism of this type:

Major Premise:	All men are mortal.
Minor Premise:	A statue is not mortal.
Conclusion:	A statue is not a man.

So far the categorical syllogism has been discussed. However, there are two other types of syllogisms that are worthy of mention. The **disjunctive syllogism** is a deductive argument that sets up a dilemma and forces the acceptance of one of the two options by eliminating or affirming one of them. An example of a disjunctive syllogism is as follows.

Major Premise:	Either War or Peace
Minor Premise:	Not Peace
Conclusion:	War

The key to the disjunctive syllogism is that the major premise must be a situation in which there are truly only two options. *War or peace* presents such a situation (of course that depends on how you define each). If an advocate were to argue that either we will have high inflation or a severe depression, that would be a false statement because there are many other options.

Valid but Untrue Disjunctive Syllogism:

Major Premise:	Either we will face high inflation or a severe depression.
Minor Premise:	We will not face high inflation.
Conclusion:	We will face a severe depression.

The above statement is false because we could have mild depression or mild inflation or a steady economy.

In addition to the requirement for the major premise to present a situation in which there are but two options, the major premise must also present two mutually exclusive items. If you argued that we may either go to the movies or go out to dinner, you would be presenting options that are not mutually exclusive. In other words, provided you had sufficient funds, you could do both. Therefore, there is no reason to advance to the minor premise in order to exclude or affirm one of the options.

Just as with the categorical syllogism, truth in the disjunctive syllogism is determined by evaluating the premises. In order to be valid, however, a disjunctive syllogism must either affirm or deny one of the options. Validity is checked by adhering to the following format:

Deny Option:

Major Premise:	A or B
Minor Premise:	Not A
Conclusion:	B

OR

Major Premise:	A or B
Minor Premise:	Not B
Conclusion:	A

Affirm Option:

Major Premise:	A or B
Minor Premise:	B
Conclusion:	Not A

OR

Major Premise:	A or B
Minor Premise:	A
Conclusion:	Not B

The final type of syllogism is the **conditional syllogism**. The conditional syllogism is an "if-then" argument. The two valid forms are as follows:

Major Premise:	If A then B
Minor Premise:	A
Conclusion:	B

OR

Major Premise:	If A then B
Minor Premise:	Not B
Conclusion:	Not A

Notice that the minor premise must either affirm the antecedent or deny the consequent. And when that happens the conclusion must also be an affirmation or a denial.

An understanding of syllogisms can be helpful when approaching the non-policy affirmative case. If you view the conclusion to a categorical or conditional syllogism as the resolution, you can see how effective this approach can be. The major premise is the criterion, and the minor premise the application of the criterion. Look at the following example on a topic that says, "Resolved: That a constitutional amendment restricting abortion would be desirable:"

Major Premise:	(Criterion) Anything that protects human life is desirable.
Minor Premise:	(Application) A constitutional amendment restricting abortion would protect human life.
Conclusion:	(Resolution) A constitutional amendment restricting abortion would be desirable.

Of course, an affirmative case based on this approach would need to define terms and defend each of the premises as true. When dealing with transcendental values, such as human life, often that is a difficult task. However, in order to defend the premises of an affirmative case, we must turn to a discussion of inductive argument. For, it is through the use of inductive argument that you will defend the major and minor premise.

Inductive Reasoning

"If it's not a deductive argument, it must be an inductive one" is a statement that may not be too far from the truth. Inductive reasoning is the use of some evidence to infer a conclusion, but inductive reasoning is not conclusive. Many logicians prefer to describe inductive reasoning as a **patterning**. If you look at events or people in a number of circumstances, patterns develop. Francis Bacon believed that the ability to use this type of patterning is at the root of genius. For example, Sigmund Freud, the father of modern psychology, observed his few children and patients to find patterns in human nature. Those patterns, as described by Freud, now serve as the basis for an entire discipline.

By using inductive argument to support your criterion (major premise) and application (minor premise), you can develop superior argumentation. In the example given above about the constitutional amendment restricting abortion, you would need to support the criterion, human life, by using inductive argument. One way to do that would be by use of examples. You could cite other examples in the contemporary world that support the major premise. You might use the example of how our society enhances law and order to protect the average citizen from harm, including the protection from murder. You might demonstrate how the U.S. spends billions of dollars on defense in order to prevent war and thus to prevent the widespread loss of human life. In other words, you are giving credence to the notion that "anything that protects human life is desirable." Notice that the arguments in support of the criterion have nothing to do with abortion itself. That is because the criterion is often a general standard, which is only later applied to the specific instance of abortion. But that same standard could be applied to any topic dealing with human life, such as capital punishment or euthanasia.

But why should debaters worry about supporting the major premise at all? It is important to check our major premises inductively because failure to do so all but guarantees poor reasoning. For instance, one of the sources of prejudice and stereotyping is the failure to check the truth of the major premise. The following unchecked syllogism demonstrates the harm that may result:

Major Premise:	All Americans are lazy.
Minor Premise:	John is an American.
Conclusion:	John is lazy.

Notice that this syllogism is a valid but untrue one. The reason it is untrue is because the arguer failed to check his or her major premise inductively. Had that double check been done, the stereotype could have been avoided, because many counter examples of work-aholic Americans could be found. You could substitute Americans in the above example for any given race or religion or human classification and come up with the same results.

The fact of the matter is everyone of us engages in stereotyping. To avoid insanity, we must generalize. Otherwise, every time we opened a can of corn, we'd have to study every kernel to determine if it fits a book's description of a corn kernel. Every time you walked into a college classroom, you would wander around until someone told you to sit down, take out some note-taking material, face the teacher, and listen to him or her. So our ability to generalize is necessary in order to function. However, where it matters (when human beings are involved for instance), we must double-check our major premises inductively. Every time we are confronted with disconfirming information we must make an effort to cross check it with any general premises we now have about the particular classification. The ability to think critically depends greatly upon our ability to adapt to new information. Ralph Waldo Emerson once remarked that "consistency is the hobgoblin of little minds," meaning that human beings must be able to change their minds if data dictate doing so.

Unfortunately, human beings are not extremely adept at knowing what disconfirming information is. Information is often misinterpreted and forced to fit existing hypotheses or major premises. For example, if a racist individual were to see disconfirming information about a prejudged race, that person would see what he or she wanted to see. An instance of this would be if a Black person were to exhibit intelligence and dynamism, a racist person would still see stupidity and lack of charisma. A related alternative would be to create a subgroup or to deny that the Black person were actually Black. After a discussion about this in an argumentation class, an Hispanic student told the class that his fraternity brothers thought he was Hawaiian, not Hispanic, simply because he didn't exhibit the stereotypical characteristics of Hispanics, such as having an accent and being poor. Abraham Kaplan, in his book, *The Conduct of Inquiry*, explains, "We see what we expect to see, what we believe we have every reason for seeing. . ."

Failing to fall into this trap is really a key to thinking critically. As Howard Kahane says, "failure to bring a world view [major premise] into conformity with experience renders cogent reasoning less likely. . ." Darley and Gross completed a study that was done with grade-school children. The conclusion of that study showed that regardless of how well welfare children performed various scholastic tasks, people perceived the welfare children to be less skilled than their upper-middle class counterparts. In other words, if a behavior does not fit into someone's hypothesis (or major premise) of how a member of a certain group should perform (all welfare children perform poorly in school), the biased individual subconsciously alters his or her perception of the behavior (excellent work is perceived as mediocre) to fit the stereotype (existing major premises).

Even college students are not exempt from this trap. Numerous studies have been done proving that college students have cluster beliefs about various races, religions, and other classifications. For example, Gergen and Gergen in 1981 reveal that many Blacks as well other college students believed the following cluster beliefs about Blacks: that they are "superstitious, lazy, happy-go-lucky, musical, and ostentatious." Believing that "all Blacks are lazy" is hardly a belief for a college-educated person to have.

This little digression hopefully convinced the reader of the importance of the inductive side of reasoning. Clearly, it is important for us to check the truth of our major premises. That concept should be employed by the beginning advocate in non-policy debate when supporting criteria and building affirmative cases. An unsupported criterion is a *prima facie* issue for the simple reason that valid-but-untrue claims can be advanced otherwise. Unsupported criteria come in other ways besides the basic assertion. Often, debaters will propose the on-balance criterion. On balance is not a standard or criterion, but it is merely a means to employ a standard. On balance in terms of what? Human life? Health? National security? The on-balance criterion is nothing more than a failure to understand the true purpose of a criterion.

CLASSIFICATIONS OF ARGUMENT

Now that you have a better understanding of deductive and inductive reasoning, a discussion of the types and tests of argument is necessary. Some of these classifications of argument may at times be deductive, at times inductive, and at times a little of both. Additionally, just because the questions asked about each type of reasoning seem objective the answers are not necessarily so. For argument types that use inductive reasoning, the application of the tests may be debatable. That is why you need to be able to defend your arguments as good ones. For instance, someone may argue that you haven't a sufficient number of examples. You must be prepared to argue that you do have a sufficient number and be able to provide additional examples.

Toulmin Analysis

In order to discuss the types of argument, an understanding of Toulmin analysis is important. Stephen Toulmin is an English philosopher whose main purpose in developing his model was to find application for logic outside the realm of the philosopher's P's and Q's. While he has failed to convince many of his philosophy colleagues, his ideas have found a home among rhetoric and argumentation scholars. The main purpose of the Toulmin model as used in argumentation is to demonstrate the structure of any given argument. The purpose of the model is not to determine validity. Toulmin analysis is analysis in its literal form: to separate an argument into its component parts. Toulmin argues that there are six elements present in any wholly explicit argument. Claim, data, and warrant are the primary components. Whenever a Toulmin analysis is completed, these three elements always must be discussed.

The first primary element, the **claim**, is the conclusion that the arguer is trying to advance. There are five basic types of claims advanced in non-policy debate: definition, fact, value, quasi-policy and policy. These have all been defined in previous chapters.

The **data** are the support for that conclusion. That support can come in the form of testimony, examples, statistics, analogies, causes, signs and definitions. Austin Freeley lists the tests for credible evidence (data) as the following:

Is there enough evidence?
Is the evidence clear?
Is the evidence consistent with other known evidence?
Is the evidence consistent within itself?
Is the evidence verifiable?
Is the source of the evidence competent?
Is the source of the evidence unprejudiced?
Is the source of the evidence reliable?
Is the evidence an index of what we need to know?
Is the evidence statistically sound?
Is the evidence the most recent available?
Is the evidence cumulative?

The **warrant** is the logical connecting link between the data and the claim. More often than not the warrant is implied, not stated, by the arguer. The warrant is the underlying assumption that one must accept in order to agree with the argument's conclusion. Remember, the warrant represents the arguer's assumption, not yours. If you disagree with the assumption, that disagreement may not be voiced by you until the Toulmin analysis is completed. For inductive reasoning, the warrant helps make the inference to the conclusion. Usually, the inductive warrant will simply assume the argument meets the key tests for that particular type of argument. For instance, the warrant for example argument is almost always the same: that the data are sufficient and typical enough to justify the claim. (Discovering whether there are sufficient and typical examples is the key to testing example argument.) On the other hand, for a deductive argument, often the warrant is simply the major premise to a syllogism. In looking at the Socrates syllogism studied earlier, the conclusion to the syllogism is the claim, *Socrates is mortal*; the minor premise is the data, *Socrates is a man*; and the major premise is the warrant, *All men are mortal*. When human beings speak, however, we usually do not speak in complete syllogisms. We normally speak in what are called enthymemes, which are bits and pieces of syllogisms. Often, the major premise and, less often, other parts of the syllogism are left out. Therefore, performing a Toulmin analysis on an enthymeme is often more difficult than a full syllogism. Additionally, for an argument by definition, which is basically deductive, the definition itself becomes the warrant.

The last three parts of the Toulmin model, the qualifier, reservation, and backing are the auxiliary parts of the model. When completing a Toulmin analysis, these elements only need to be included if the author includes them him or herself. However, the refuter may want to introduce these elements if the arguer fails to verbalize them. The **qualifier** establishes the degree of cogency of the argument, as explicitly stated by the arguer. The qualifier manifests itself usually as one word or phrase, such as probably, certainly, perhaps, more than likely, possibly, plausibly, rarely, hardly ever, by no means, and so on. The **reservation** is a specific exception to the claim, such as "Mr. Jones says, 'it will rain tomorrow, *unless the wind picks up*.'" "Unless the wind picks up" is the exception (reservation) to the claim, "it will rain tomorrow." The **backing** is support for the warrant. If challenged, the advocate often has to provide backing to maintain a high degree of cogency with regard to a particular argument. As an example of backing, the arguer above might indicate that Mr. Jones has correctly predicted the weather the past 100 days straight. That would support the warrant that Mr. Jones is an expert on the subject of weather and is unbiased.

The Toulmin analysis is best when visualized in its proper form:

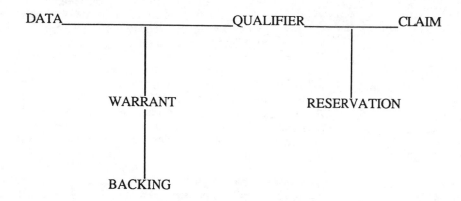

Testimony Argument

An argument from testimony is an argument that uses as its support the authority of another person. If someone were to say, "Mr. Jones said that it will rain tomorrow," the support for that argument is Mr. Jones' authority. Therefore, that argument is an argument from testimony or authority.

Testimony argument is by nature secondary. A person other than the primary source is using a quotation or paraphrase as grounds for a particular claim. Let's look at a complete version of the above argument:

Mr. Jones says that it probably will rain tomorrow unless the wind picks up. Mr. Jones has predicted correctly the weather the past 100 days straight.

The Toulmin analysis is as follows:

Claim:	It will rain tomorrow.
Data:	Mr. Jones says so.
Warrant:	Mr. Jones is an expert on the subject and is unbiased.
Qualifier:	Probably.
Reservation:	Unless the wind picks up.
Backing:	Mr. Jones has predicted correctly the weather the past 100 days straight.

Notice that the arguer stated everything explicitly except for the warrant. Remember, the warrant is the underlying assumption that the arguer makes, and it is usually unstated. The other five elements must be explicitly stated in order to be included.

The warrant for any testimony argument is basically the same as the one listed above. In order to determine the warrant for an argument, you must first classify the argument. In this case, that is given to you: This is a testimony argument. The second step, in this case, is to assume that the argument meets the key tests for that particular type of argument. The tests for testimony argument are as follows:

1. Is the source an expert?
2. Is the source an expert on the subject being discussed?
3. Is the source unbiased?

Once you identify the warrant in a debate round, you need to evaluate those tests and answer them for yourself. Remember, answering the questions on your own is not a part of Toulmin analysis *per se*. For the first test listed above, an advocate must determine whether the source has the expertise necessary even to be considered. Often, in a debate round, an opponent may quote a law-school student or a graduate student. Of course, your opponent may not readily admit the fact that his or her evidence was written by an apprentice. That's why you need to ask to see the qualifications of any unqualified evidence. Occasionally, an opponent will read evidence from an obscure newspaper or magazine with little or no journalistic expertise. In either of these cases, the testimony fails to meet the first test for testimony argument. Of course, your opponent may be ready to defend the evidence as presented, and the defense may be justified. Remember the caution listed above: Just because the tests seem objective does not mean the answers are necessarily so. In other words, it is arguable whether a law-school student lacks expertise. On the one hand, he or she is still studying and hasn't completed an education nor received proper credentials. On the other hand, a second-year law school student who has an article published in the *Yale Law Journal* can hardly be considered a lay source. These tests are not scientific litmus papers that will turn a certain color if a person is an expert or unbiased or whatever. These tests merely provide the a format for evaluating a line of argument. They are not meant to end all controversy.

If, however, you do establish that the source is an expert, you must then ask the second question. The second test for testimony argument is to ask whether the expertise is related to the claim. In other words, we may accept the law student's expertise, but the claim may be dealing with whether there would be a nuclear winter after a missile exchange between two countries. Obviously, the credentials, law, have nothing to do with the claim, effects of a nuclear war.

The third test for testimony argument is to ask whether the source of the information is unbiased. Realize, again, that bias is not a black/white issue. There are degrees of bias, so whether a source is too biased to be acceptable can be argued in a debate round. Take the issue of whether communist countries harm human rights. Say you have two sources each saying that communist countries do not harm human rights: one from a member of the communist party and one from a liberal democrat in the U.S. Senate. Obviously, the communist party member would be viewed as much more biased than a liberal democrat. Yet both have clear biases. Although the politician is biased, an advocate could make a case for him or her more easily than for the communist party member.

On the other hand, if a source goes against a perceived bias, then that evidence may even more valuable. Say Ronald Reagan were to state publicly that Reaganomics is an unworkable economic theory. We would expect Reagan to be biased in favor of his previous policies. By using evidence that goes against a perceived bias, therefore, we may actually strengthen our position.

Example Argument

Example argument provides the patterning process that is inductive argument. As mentioned, when supporting major premises, often you want to use example argument to do so. **Perfect induction** comprises looking at all of the examples within a given classification or population in order to find the patterns or similarities within the grouping. Often, however, perfect induction is not possible.

When perfect induction is not possible, certain rules must be applied to the data to determine if they are acceptable. The tests for example argument are as follows:

1. Are the examples relevant to the claim?
2. Are there a sufficient number of examples?
3. Are the examples typical?
4. Are counter examples insignificant?
5. Is the claim qualified?

Note that the first question deals with relevancy. This is a question that is asked about a number of different types of argument. It is a more general question than the rest. It is simply asking if the data and the claim are related enough even to consider. If you answer "no" to the first question, there is little reason to ask the other questions.

For instance, an advocate may advance an argument which says that many politicians are corrupt. As data, the advocate provides the example of a U.S. Senator's support of a congressional pay raise. One may be able to advance the argument that support of a pay raise is indicative of a politician's greed and thus corruption. However, just because you ask for a raise does not mean that you are corrupt. Therefore, the example (a senator asking for a pay raise) is not relevant to the claim (many politicians are corrupt). Another factor in determining relevancy is the issue of time. For instance, an advocate could argue that moral decay exists in U.S. society. As data, the debater may offer the example of the sexual revolution. Arguably, however, the sexual revolution is irrelevant because it occurred in the 1960's, and the A.I.D.S. epidemic today has all but curbed any continuing revolution.

The second question, *are there a sufficient number of examples?*, is a question that cannot be answered with any surety. Statisticians have developed formulas to determine a sufficient sample size for a given population. Outside the realm of statistics, the answer to this question, then, is subjective, and should be considered at the same time as the third question, *typical examples*. For instance, an advocate may advance the claim that the forest service harvests too much timber on U.S. national forests. As support for the claim, the advocate offers the example of Lassen National Forest in northeastern California. In answering the question about sufficient numbers of examples, on the surface, this one example out of all of the National Forests in the country would seem insufficient. However, you must also ask the question about whether the example is typical, because, if all of the other national forests harvest the same percentage of timber, then one example may be sufficient. There are two ways to determine whether an example is typical. One way is to use example argument in conjunction with general testimony argument. For instance, you might use the example of the Lassen Forest with a quotation from a U.S. Senator saying that the forest service harvests too much timber from the national forests. A second way to indicate an example is typical, of course, is to provide more examples. So the relationship between sufficiency and "typicality" becomes apparent. One example is sufficient if it's typical, but often we don't know if it's typical unless we look at numerous examples. Hence, using simple example argument often puts the advocate in a dilemma. The best option is to use example argument in conjunction with general testimony argument, as suggested above.

The fourth question, *are the counter examples insignificant?*, is related to the last two questions as well. Rarely will you find a classification or population with 100 percent similarity or patterning. Of course, that means that there will always be a counter example, even with a seemingly sound example argument. Therefore, as you are trying to defend your examples as sufficient and typical, you also must be able to refute any counter examples raised by your opponents. In the above instance, your opponent may point out that in the Mendocino National Forest, timber harvests were cut in half last year. Your duty, then, is to prove that Mendocino is not a typical example. In this instance, you may be able to find evidence that says that the spotted owl population in the Mendocino Forest is unusually large, and court battles have prevented many timber sales there; therefore the Mendocino Forest is atypical. You must be aware of as many possible counter examples, such as this, so that you can quickly dismiss them.

The final question, *is the claim qualified?*, refers to the fact that, with anything other than perfect induction, example argument cannot provide 100 percent certainty. The best we can expect, then, is an argument that establishes a high degree of probability. Therefore, qualifiers (such as *probably*, *more than likely*, *many*, or *most*) ought to be affixed to a claim established by example argument. This again goes back to the issue of stereotyping. Any black/white views that we have about the world ought to be suspect simply from the standpoint that we cannot know everything.

The warrant for an example argument assumes that the examples meet the above tests. Remember, that the listener is not making that assumption; the arguer is. Once the Toulmin analysis is completed, you may then evaluate the warrant, which may call for backing. Let's look at the following example:

> The U.S. national forests are probably being over harvested. Look at Lassen National Forest; they take way too much timber out of that place. And Lassen is of average size and use of most forests in the national forest system. Well, I suppose this is all true unless Lassen has some kind of one-time harvest plan going.

The Toulmin analysis should look like this:

Claim:	The U.S. national forests are being over harvested.
Data:	Look at Lassen National Forest; they take way too much timber out of that place.
Warrant:	Lassen is a typical and sufficient example to prove the claim.
Qualifier:	Probably.
Reservation:	Unless Lassen has some kind of one-time harvest plan going.
Backing:	Lassen is of average size and use.

Notice that again that the warrant is unstated by the arguer. The warrant, as implied by the arguer, merely assumes that the argument meets the key tests for example reasoning. Once the Toulmin has been completed, however, you may then evaluate the warrant. In this case, you may in fact find the assumption faulty. Indeed, Lassen may be atypical.

Statistics

Statistics involve the use of numbers: conclusions to studies, results of opinion polls, or total numbers of people or objects within a certain classification. The one thing that you should gain from any discussion on statistics is that debate advocates ought to know the methodology of any study or poll that they use. Sometimes that is difficult, however. Often, a study's conclusion is found in a magazine or in some other secondary source. Whenever possible, look for the the primary source, so that if you are challenged, you may defend a particular methodology. In the course of your research, you may come across hundreds of studies found in secondary sources. Obviously, you may not have the time or the inclination to locate the primary source for each study; however, the studies that seem important to you or that you use for an affirmative case or value objection you really ought to locate and read. Debaters raise four common issues with regard to statistics: the degree of cogency assigned by the study's author(s), the sampling technique used in the study, the means employed to find central tendency, and whether the conclusions are compared to other figures.

In the first case, those who perform studies usually have a good idea of what they want to say about the data. Often a conclusion to a study might include a caution, such as, "the data are useful only for the population under study and are not generalizable." Such a statement means that the study's conclusion is extremely limited. Use of such a study for debate evidence must be considered carefully. During the third-parties in presidential elections topic, some affirmative teams used inoculation theory to prove that more participation by third parties will cause the general public to reject them. Inoculation theory is a medical analogy that says that unless we have been inoculated against a diseased argument, we may fall victim to it when we are weakened and exposed. Thus, affirmatives argued that third party participation is beneficial because it eliminates the possibility that in times of crisis a radical third party candidate would be elected to the presidency or to any other office. Negative teams quickly armed themselves with indictments against the inoculation studies, saying that the studies were not generalizable. Many affirmative teams were not ready for the indictments and had not read their own studies. Had they done so, they would have realized that inoculation theory was intended to be generalizable for the cultural truisms that third parties threatened, but not for other matters.

A second consideration when using statistics is the sampling technique employed in the study. Cable networks are infamous for asking callers to phone a 900 number in order to give their opinions on various subjects. However, the networks usually offer the qualification that the survey is not scientific, but only represents the opinions of the callers who decide to participate. If a debater attempted to cite the conclusion to a 900-number survey, the opposing team should point out that such a survey does not generate a **random sample** of the population and thus may not be used as evidence. A random sample suggests simply that each person in a given population has an equal chance of being surveyed. Some studies take that a step further to obtain a **representative sample.** To do that, certain segments of the population are isolated, and the survey insures that it obtains a proportionate amount of responses from each segment. For instance, if you were doing a study of freshman, sophomores, juniors, and seniors at your college, you would need to guarantee that you had a relatively proportionate number of people from each class level respond to your survey. **Sample size** is also a consideration. If a poll only contacted 13 people out of a population of one million, obviously, the sample size would be too small. The **questioning technique** may also have a bearing on whether the results are usable. A survey, for example, may ask whether a college student has ever been treated for a sexually transmitted disease, and 38 percent may have answered, "yes." In a debate round, an advocate may present the results as, "38 percent of the students on our college campuses have a sexually transmitted disease." Obviously, that number is inflated because many of those who affirmed that they had been treated may have been cured; thus, they may no longer have the disease. The questions themselves may be flawed, as well. A survey on dreams and dreaming may ask respondents if they have ever *floundered* in their sleep. That question is vague because the word, *floundered,* could be defined any number of different ways. Therefore, any results compiled from that question would be useless.

The third common concern voiced about statistics is the means employed to determine central tendency. There are three ways to determine central tendency in a group of numbers: mean, median, and mode. Each of these methods may render a completely different result, so choosing one over another may benefit the arguer. Certainly, as consumers of argument, we must be aware of the differences.

Mean refers to the mathematical average. This is the same as the averaging that you did in elementary school. You take the sum total of a group of numbers and divide by *n*. Median seems to be the most preferred by statisticians for providing the most accurate picture of central tendency. Median is merely the number that falls in the middle of a group of numerically listed numbers. If you have an even amount of numbers, you use the mathematical average of the two middle numbers. For instance, for the list of numbers, 2, 3, 4, **5**, 6, 7, 10, the median would be 5. There are seven numbers total, three numbers less than *five* and three numbers greater than *five*. Hence, *five* is the median, falling in the

middle of that group of seven numbers. Mode seems to be the least preferred method of
generating central tendency. Mode is simply the number appearing most often in a group
of numbers. For list of numbers, 1, 2, 3, 4, 5, 6, 7, 7, 7, obviously the mode would be 7.
The undesirable nature of the mode becomes apparent in this example because *seven* is no
where near the "center" of that group of numbers.

The cost of housing is a good example of where methods of discovering central
tendency are misused. As a simplified example let's say that we had a neighborhood with
the following housing values:

$600,000.00	Mode: $600,000.
$600,000.00	
$600,000.00	
$300,000.00	
$250,000.00	Mean: $214,000.
$ 98,000.00	
$ 89,000.00	Median: $87,000.
$ 85,000.00	
$ 78,000.00	
$ 76,000.00	
$ 67,000.00	
$ 55,000.00	
$ 53,000.00	
$ 45,000.00	

In this example, the mean is $214,000.; the median is $87,000.; the mode is
$600,000. Clearly, there is a marked difference between the three outcomes. If you were
deciding whether to move into a particular neighborhood, it would be difficult to decide that
if you were given the figure of $600,000. or even $214,000. as the cost of housing.
However, for a person minimally qualified to buy a home, the $87,000. median figure is
much more palatable, and much more representative of the cost of the housing listed. Nine
of the fourteen houses listed are under $100.000. Although this example is hypothetical, it
does represent the characteristics of many numerical factors, such as annual income, auto
prices, professional athletes' salaries, or the yearly intake of pork fat.

A final consideration is that numbers in themselves do not often tell the entire tale.
Yet, our culture has taught us that numbers do not lie. So, we are caught between what we
do not know and what we have been taught. The rule of thumb is that a single number
usually needs to be compared to something else. For instance, if someone were to argue
that your college student population has too many people on academic probation. And they
give the proof that 150 students are currently in such a situation. One hundred and fifty
certainly seems like a lot of students. However, 150 compared to what? If your college
has 15,000 students, 150 is only one percent of the student body. What if the national
average were three percent? If so, the 150 figure may actually be low, not high.

Toulmin analysis for statistical argument is problematic because the tests and rules
for statistics fill volumes. So to say that the warrant assumes the argument meets the key
tests would make the warrant for any statistical argument volumes long. To simplify
matters simply list the warrant as an assumption that the statistical methodology is sound.
If the study is a survey, you may want to indicate that the sample size is sufficient and the
sample was randomly produced. If the study is an experiment, you may want to indicate
that the study is externally valid (generalizable), and so on. On the other hand, if you are
making an inference from the statistical information, then the warrant is easier. Then, you
simply state that the statistical information is a good indication of what you want to know.
For instance, an argument could be built using the above housing information:

The average price of a home in this neighborhood is $214,000. Therefore, I probably can't afford to buy a home here, unless the median price is a better indicator.

The Toulmin analysis might proceed as follows:

Claim:	I can't afford to buy a home here.
Data:	The average price of a home is $214.000.
Warrant:	The mean price of a home is a good indicator of ability to pay.
Qualifier:	Probably.
Reservation:	Unless the median price is a better indicator.
Backing:	None.

Analogy Argument

An **analogy** is a comparison of two things to make a descriptive or argumentative point. A **figurative analogy** is used to make a descriptive point. A figurative analogy may not be used as an argumentative tool because the instances compared are too different to establish a high level of probability. Comparing our membership in the United Nations with getting a car repaired is an example of a figurative analogy. The two items, membership in an international organization and repair of a car, are items from different classifications. The key to identifying a figurative analogy is that the items are just that, from different classifications. Figurative analogies are effective tools for explaining a difficult point. In fact, some of the greatest public speakers throughout history have used figurative analogies to convey complex concepts. However, the first rule in determining valid analogy reasoning is to exclude all figurative analogies from consideration.

Literal analogies, on the other hand, may be used to establish a high level of probability. Literal analogies compare items from the same classification. College A and college B for instance are items from the same classification: colleges. Therefore, a comparison of college A and college B would provide the framework necessary for a literal analogy. Any two items within the same classification provide the same framework: two trees, two houses, two cars, two hot air balloons, two cities, two countries, two military campaigns, two advertising blitzes, two argumentation courses, and so on.

The simple fact that the analogies are from the same classification of things alone does not guarantee a sound argument. The analogies must also be similar in significant detail. You may argue for instance that the type of student government at Maple College would work well at Oakwood College. Obviously, comparing two colleges meets the first test of insuring a literal analogy. However, in order to meet the second test, you would need to establish that Maple and Oakwood were similar in detail: private, 5,000 or fewer students, well funded student government, etc. If this is true, you may move to the third test for analogy reasoning.

The third test asks the advocate to determine whether there are critical differences that deny the comparison. For instance, you may compare the world court to the U.S. Supreme Court. Certainly, the analogy meets the first test: they are both courts and thus are in the same classification. They are also similar in significant detail: both have justices, both render decisions, and both promulgate their decisions to their respective constituencies. However, when you apply the third test, you find a critical difference that denies the comparison: the U.S. Supreme Court's decisions are binding; the world court's decisions are advisory. So if you were to argue that what works for the U.S. Supreme Court would work for the world court, you may be committing a fallacy of analogy reasoning.

To review, the tests for analogy reasoning are as follows:

1. Are only literal analogies used?
2. Are the instances similar in significant detail?
3. Are the differences noncritical?

An analogy warrant, of course, would assume the argument meets these tests. Notice also that the questions are progressive. In other words, if you answer "no" to any of them, there is really little need to continue to the next test; the analogy must be considered invalid if a *no* answer to but one question appears obvious.

An argument may be presented as follows:

The Gotham City program to reduce rat infestation should also work in the city of Oz. The Gotham program reduced rat sightings by 50 percent.

The Toulmin analysis should proceed accordingly:

Claim:	The Gotham City program to reduce rat infestation should also work in the city of Oz.
Data:	The Gotham program reduced rat sightings by 50 percent.
Warrant:	Gotham and Oz are similar in significant detail and their differences are noncritical.
Qualifier:	None.
Reservation:	None.
Backing:	None.

Causal   Argument

Causal argument suggests that some instance or event forces, gives rise to, or helps produce a particular effect. There are two types of causal argument. **Cause-to-effect argument** occurs when the advocate knows the cause and is projecting what the effect will be. Usually, this is a present-to-future argument. Many arguments on quasi-policy topics are cause-to-effect. On the nuclear-freeze-is-desirable topic, advocates argued that the known cause (nuclear freeze) would produce desirable, but unknown, effects (peace, reduced threat of nuclear war, *etc.*). Through fiat power (the power of the affirmative to implement policies hypothetically so that they may be evaluated by the advocates), the nuclear freeze occurs hypothetically during the debate round (the present). The debate focuses on what the effects (the future) of that policy change would be.

Effect-to-cause arguments, as the name suggests, are the exact opposite of a cause-to-effect argument. Here, you look at a present effect which is known, and you project into the past to try to determine an unknown, but suspected, cause. You may also work from a past effect (World War II) to an earlier cause (the suspected cause or causes of World War II). If there were a world-wide catastrophe tomorrow, you can bet that the world's leaders would all be engaged in effect-to-cause argument, trying to determine how such an event could have occurred.

Regardless of which type of causal argument employed, the tests for both are the same:

1. Is the cause relevant to the effect?
2. Is the cause an inherent factor in producing the effect?
3. Are there any counter-causes that may prevent the effect?

The first question is the on the most basic of levels: Is the cause relevant to the effect? Many people read horoscopes because they believe that the position of the stars at birth causes one to have a certain disposition and destiny. However, scientific data reject such a causal relationship. The position of the stars at birth has absolutely nothing to do with a person's fate. The cause is not relevant to the effect. Similarly, some people believe that walking underneath a ladder will bring bad luck. Again, a person's physical position *vis a vis* a ladder really is irrelevant to the effect, bad luck. It may not be intelligent to walk under a ladder, since something may fall on you, but, beyond that, there is no relevancy. Some people have held that the stock market crash in 1929 caused the great depression. In answering whether the crash and the depression are relevant, one may have to say, "yes." At least, it is possible that the one caused the other. Both instances are economic in nature. Both instances had global repercussions.

In answering the second question as to whether the cause is an inherent factor in producing the effect, you may have a different answer. The stock market crash might have been also an effect of the same economic downturn, not the cause. In other words, the alleged cause may not be an inherent factor in producing the effect. Another example of a relevant, but not inherent cause is the A.I.D.S. controversy. Some people fear that casual contact with an A.I.D.S. victim may cause transmittance of the disease. Certainly, person to person contact is relevant to transmitting a disease, but in this case it is not inherent. To date, there is no documented instance of casual contact resulting in A.I.D.S. being transmitted. Therefore, the alleged cause (casual contact) is not an inherent factor in producing the effect (A.I.D.S. transmission). Whereas, the relevancy test asks whether the causal relationship is possible, the inherency test asks whether the causal relationship is probable. In asking either of these first two questions, realize that one-to-one causal relationships are rare. The world presents a system of interdependencies. One cause may affect the system, but the system is not predictable completely. Therefore, be wary of one-to-one causal arguments.

The final test asks whether any counter-causes exist to prevent the effect. Suppose you argued that a unilateral nuclear freeze would lead to world peace. However, the opposing team in turn argued that a unilateral freeze would leave other countries with no incentive to negotiate with us. Therefore, in the long run, a freeze may postpone important arms negotiations and actually fuel the arms race. You would need to argue that no such counter-cause would exist, and that a more likely scenario would be for other countries to cure any economic woes by similarly freezing production and deployment of nuclear arms.

For the purposes of a Toulmin analysis, a causal argument might run something like this:

There probably will be a great depression in the 1990's, unless we do something now. Economic disparity between the rich and the poor has increased. The distancing has become greater. The greater the disparity, the greater the chance for economic catastrophe.

The Toulmin analysis would look something like this:

Claim:	There will be a great depression in the 1990's.
Data:	The economic disparity between the rich and the poor has increased.
Warrant:	Economic disparity is a relevant, inherent, and sufficient cause of depression.
Qualifier:	Probably.
Reservation:	Unless we do something now.
Backing:	The greater the disparity, the greater the chance for economic catastrophe.

Sign   Argument

Sign argument serves as the basis for the medical profession. When you have a cold, you don't see the cold virus; you see the symptoms or signs of the virus: clogged sinuses, runny nose, sore throat, nagging cough, and aching head. When a doctor diagnoses someone with A.I.D.S., the doctor does not see the A.I.D.S. virus, but rather he or she runs a test to determine whether the patient has the antibodies for the A.I.D.S. virus. The presence of the A.I.D.S. antibodies is a sign that the person has A.I.D.S. The legal profession also relies to some extent on sign or circumstantial argument. You are sitting in your car on the side of the road at 2 am with a blood alcohol level of .20, and your engine is hot, keys in the ignition, and there are no empty bottles of alcohol for miles around. A police officer stopping by would surely arrest you for drunken driving. All of the circumstances in which that officer finds you serve as signs that you had been driving while intoxicated.

In a debate round, sign argument plays an important role as well. A sign argument is an argument in which two variables are linked inherently, so that if one is present, the other is also; if one is missing, the other is also missing. Many events or circumstances serve as signs that some other event or circumstance exists. Conversely, the absence of certain events or circumstances serve as signs that some other event or circumstance is absent. The tests for sign argument are as follows:

1. Is the known variable relevant to the unknown variable?
2. Is the sign relationship inherent?

The first test, relevancy, asks whether the sign relationship is merely possible. If the U.S. sent a large regiment of soldiers to Honduras, it would be possible that we were going to attack a bordering country.   Therefore, the variables are relevant to each other. However, if we applied the second test to determine if the sign relationship were inherent, we would find that it is not. The presence of additional U.S. troops in any given country usually does not mean attack. We simply may be performing military maneuvers or merely deterring a bordering country's possible aggression. Therefore, the sign relationship is relevant, but not inherent.

On the other hand, say an advocate were to argue that the Soviet Union did not plan to attack Western Europe. As proof, the advocate read evidence explaining that the Soviets have not crossed the border in over 40 years, that the Soviets have recently withdrawn many soldiers from Eastern European countries, and that the Soviets have allowed the democratization of the Warsaw-Pact Nations. These signs certainly are relevant to the suspected variable that the Soviets do not plan to attack Western Europe, but is the sign relationship inherent? The answer is "yes." If a country were planning an attack, it certainly would not withdraw troops from the future front. If anything, that country would amass troops on the border.   Let's evaluate a sign argument using the Toulmin analysis:

It definitely is going to rain tomorrow. There is a rainbow ring around the moon, and the crickets are chirping wildly.

Claim:	It is going to rain tomorrow.
Data:	There is a rainbow ring around the moon, and the crickets are chirping wildly.
Warrant:	These data, ring and crickets, are relevant and inherent to the claim, rain.
Qualifier:	Definitely.
Reservation:	None.
Backing:	None.

Argument by Definition

The **argument by definition** is basically a deductive argument. This type of argument determines whether something should be included within the realm of a particular definition or classification. The definitional argument then may make inferences about that classification. For instance, the drunken driving example suggested in the previous section works well here, too:

The driver had a blood alcohol level of .20 while driving in the state of California. Therefore, the driver almost certainly is guilty of driving while intoxicated, unless the breath meter was not functioning.

In completing a Toulmin analysis, the definition of *driving while intoxicated* becomes the warrant:

Claim:	The driver is guilty of driving while intoxicated.
Data:	The driver had a blood alcohol level of .20.
Warrant:	Driving while intoxicated in California is defined as having a blood alcohol level of .10 or higher while operating a motor vehicle.
Qualifier:	Almost certainly.
Reservation:	Unless the breath meter was not functioning.
Backing:	None.

SUMMARY

A debater must know how to identify and use sound reasoning. This chapter covered deductive and inductive reasoning, as well as the various forms of argument: testimony, example, statistical, analogy, cause, sign, and definition. The Toulmin model was used to reveal the structure of an argument and to discover the underlying assumptions of it. Once armed with this information, it should be easier for advocates to construct their own sound arguments and to find weaknesses in opponent's arguments. The next chapter should provide additional guidance for exposing opponent's fallacious reasoning.

6 | EXPOSING FALLACIES

The purpose of this chapter is not to give you a complete picture of all of the fallacies ever discussed. That could fill volumes. The purpose of this chapter is to provide the advocate with a brief description of the most common fallacies confronted in a non-policy debate round. Advocates must avoid using fallacies and must be able to expose fallacies committed by their opponents.

THE FALLACY OF EXAMPLE ARGUMENT

The **fallacy of example argument** is a fancy name for a misused inductive argument. In previous chapters this fallacy was also called a hasty generalization. A fallacy of example reasoning occurs when an advocate violates one of the key tests for example argument. Those key tests are as follows:

1. Are there a sufficient number of examples.
2. Are the examples typical?

Remember that these tests are not objective scientific litmus tests; nevertheless, if you feel that your opponent may have insufficient or atypical examples, it may be worth your while to press the point. Say that your opponent argues that people have their medical privacy violated due to unprotected computer data banks. Your opponent argues further that this violation of privacy is harmful. For proof, your opponent offers a single example of Mr. Magoo who lost his job because his company's management discovered, through unprotected medical data banks, that he had been treated for a serious disease. While that is a compelling example, it is only one instance, and it may be atypical. You must challenge your opponents either to provide additional examples or to read general testimony evidence that indicates that the problem is significant. While asking for additional proof, point out that the example, as presented, is insufficient and atypical; thus, your opponent has committed a fallacy of example reasoning. Additionally, you can strengthen your position by reading evidence denying that the problem is widespread.

The fallacy of composition is a related fallacy. This fallacy holds that what is true of the parts is true always of the whole, but it fails to take into consideration the exceptions to the rule. For instance, someone might argue that, "four members of the band won national awards; therefore, all 20 band members must be fantastic." Obviously, just because a few members are exceptional does not mean that the whole is exceptional. All 20 members playing together might sound like a sick elephant.

FALLACY OF DIVISION

The fallacy of division is the opposite of the fallacy of composition. The fallacy of division is a misuse of deductive argument. This misuse occurs when the conclusion of the syllogism has the degree of cogency of certainty, while the major premise allows for exceptions. For instance if you advanced the major premise that "as a group, football players are tall and muscular," that may be true. However, when you say that John is not tall and muscular and thus cannot be a football player, you commit this fallacy. Note that the conclusion to the syllogism, "cannot be a football player," is stated with certainty. Whereas, the major premise says, "as a group." Any group of people, including a group of football players, includes individuals with unique attributes. John may very well be the fastest player ever to play college football, so he does not need to be tall or muscular.

FALLACY OF MISTAKEN CAUSATION

A fallacy of mistaken causation is a causal argument that fails to meet the key tests for causal reasoning. To review the tests for causal reasoning, they are listed here:

1. Is the cause relevant to the effect?
2. Is the cause an inherent factor in producing the effect?
3. Are there any counter-causes that may prevent the effect?

Should your opponent argue that the Bush administration's domestic policies caused third world countries to turn to communism, you would need to argue that your opponent is guilty of a fallacy of mistaken causation. In asking the first question, about whether the cause is relevant, you would have to say, "no." Without any compelling evidence to the contrary, U.S. domestic policy rarely affects a third world country's choice of political philosophy. If your opponent's argument dealt with U.S. foreign policy, then that may be a different matter altogether.

A specific causal fallacy is the fallacy of *post hoc ergo propter hoc*, which means literally "after the fact therefore because of the fact." This *post hoc* fallacy occurs when chronology becomes confused with causation. For example, Shortly after Ronald Reagan's inauguration in 1981, the Iran Hostage Crisis ended. However, just because the inauguration occurred before the hostages' release does not mean that the inauguration caused the release. To believe so, would be to fall victim to the *post hoc* fallacy. It may be true that the captors were waiting for Carter to leave office; even so, the inauguration did not cause the release. Advocates commit the *post hoc* fallacy whenever they justify causality by explaining that the alleged cause occurred before the supposed effect. Chronology does not prove causality; chronology merely makes causality possible.

THE FALLACY OF SIGNIFICANCE

The fallacy of significance refers to the use of statistics. As mentioned in the previous chapter, an advocate must compare a single statistic to another number in order to determine whether that statistic were significant. To charge that the single statistic is significant without the comparison is to commit the fallacy of significance. Recall the example from the previous chapter: 150 students on academic probation is not necessarily a lot of people on academic probation. It could be the lowest percentage ever achieved by a college in the history of post-secondary education. But of course, you cannot know that until you compared the 150 figure to other colleges past and present.

THE FALSE ANALOGY

The false analogy occurs when the tests for analogy reasoning are not followed. The tests are,

1. Are only literal analogies used?
2. Are the instances similar in significant detail?
3. Are there are any critical differences that deny the comparison?

Say your opponents argue that a homeless program works in the U.S.; therefore, it will work in Ethiopia. Obviously, there are critical differences that deny comparing the U.S. to Ethiopia. Therefore, in a debate round, you would use four-point refutation to dismiss the argument as a false analogy. Your response should proceed as follows:

1. My opponent argues that the U.S. homeless program will work in Ethiopia.

2. I argue that comparing the U.S. with Ethiopia presents a false analogy.

3. The analogy is false because there are critical differences between the U.S. and Ethiopia that deny the comparison. The governmental structure in Ethiopia and the high percentage of Ethiopians living in poverty may preclude a U.S. style program from working there.

4. Therefore, the homeless program will not work.

A PRIORI FALLACY

An **a priori fallacy** is an inability to adjust our major premises to disconfirming information. All of us have a set of values and beliefs called a world view. Each belief and value in that world view could be formed into a major premise of a syllogism. For instance, a person may have a major premise which says that "everything our country does is wrong." Then, if our country should do something right, like secure the release of a hostage, that person, rather than evaluate the event for rightness or wrongness, would immediately assign evil motives. This type of reaction relates directly with the *a priori* fallacy. Closed mind, opinionated, dogmatic, black/white view, intolerant, or even naive are all descriptive terms that could easily apply to a person who constantly commits the *a priori* fallacy.

When one enters the world of intercollegiate debate, often an advocate must rethink some issues. A communist takeover of a country for instance is not considered automatically evil. If you were to argue that U.S. policies are bad because they enhance the risk of communist takeover of third world countries, your opponent may ask you to provide a concrete harm from communist takeover. Many novice debaters are hard pressed to answer that question. Our society drills us with propaganda about how evil communism is, but that same society fails to arm most of us with the information or critical thinking skills necessary to fill a one-minute speech against communism.

The following statement illustrates the *a priori* fallacy:

John couldn't have been convicted of hit-and-run driving. He's not that kind of person. He's responsible.

In this example, the person speaking has a major premise about John that precludes John's illegal behavior. It is an *a priori* fallacy; because the arguer's prior beliefs prevent the arguer from even considering the new disconfirming information.

BEGGING THE QUESTION

The statement, "abortion is wrong because abortion is murder," is an example of the **begging the question** fallacy. The question that is being begged, "is abortion really murder?", is unanswered by the statement. In order to propose the above argument, you would need to first prove that human life begins at conception. Otherwise, abortion cannot be considered murder. This type of fallacy uses one unsupported claim to prove another. The above argument looks like this:

Unsupported claim number one: Abortion is wrong.
Unsupported claim number two: Abortion is murder.

ARGUING IN A CIRCLE

Like begging the question, **a circular argument** also employs two unsupported claims. Circular argument differs, however, because its claims reverse rolls. The following conversation demonstrates the circular nature of this fallacy:

Mary: Jesus is really God.
Joan: How do you know that?
Mary: My preacher says so.
Joan: Why does your preacher say so?
Mary: Well, because Jesus is really God, pure and simple.

The following schematic shows what is happening here:

Claim: Jesus is really God.
Data: Because my Preacher says so.

Claim: My preacher says so.
Data: Because Jesus is really God.

If your opponents become entrenched in a circular argument, you must point out that fact, and you must explain that the first unsupported claim still lacks sufficient proof. Without additional data, your opponents must lose that particular argument.

REDUCTIO AD ABSURDUM

Reductio ad absurdum is a Latin phrase, which means literally, "reducing to the absurd." Also called the fallacy of extension, the *reductio ad absurdum* fallacy has become entrenched in intercollegiate debate. Occasionally, a debater will argue something like, "if we raise the price of milk, nuclear war will result." That argument would go something like this:

I. If we raise the price of milk, catastrophic consequences will result.
    A. U.S. milk prices affect the overall food-price picture.
    B. A significant rise in food prices adversely affects the world's economy.
    C. When the world's economy is harmed, revolutions are triggered.
    D. Revolutions give rise to a means-to-end mentality.
    E. The means-to-end mentality will lead to nuclear war.

This argument is nothing but a series of cause-to-effect arguments. The more links that are added, the more unlikely the final result. Unfortunately, such an argument cannot be dismissed by simply saying that it is a fallacy. Many debate critics accept this type of argument. When refuting the fallacy of extension, focus on the weakest links. And, if you cannot destroy the links, at least show that the initial cause (in this case a rise in milk prices) is not a unique or important factor in the end result. You may also ask for examples. For instance, ask the other team to give an example of sub-point "C": "Tell me one revolution that was started solely because of a faulty world economy." If your opponents cannot answer, you have strengthened your case. If they do give an example, ask why we haven't had a nuclear war yet.

A related fallacy is **the slippery slope fallacy**. Instead of evidence supporting each link as in the fallacy of extension, the progression or slippery slope toward catastrophe is asserted. The metaphor implies that, once you take a first step, you will automatically slide all the way down the hill. A common example of the slippery slope fallacy is the warning sometimes mentioned about drugs: If you inhale one lung full of marijuana, soon you will be taking and selling hard drugs. Additionally, some Supreme Court decisions commit this fallacy, when they assert that, once a freedom is limited, sooner or later the freedom will be destroyed completely. Implication of the slippery slope fallacy does not mean that the eventual catastrophe will not occur; it just means that the conclusion is unproven. A marijuana user may very well end up a drug pusher, but the same user also may never smoke again. Slippery slope is a fallacy because the conclusion is pure speculation.

THE *AD HOMINEM* FALLACY

Ad Hominem means literally "against the man." This fallacy substitutes the person for the argument. Through desperation of not being able to respond to a particular argument, a frustrated debater may falsely accuse his or her opponents of fabricating the evidence. Not only would that be a highly serious charge, but it would also be an instance of an *ad hominem* attack. The debater focused on the person (opponent) rather than the argument. Obviously, you should never accuse your opponents of anything for which you don't have concrete proof. However, if your opponents did actually fabricate evidence, would the accusation then be an *ad hominem* attack? The answer is "no." If the accusation is germane to the issue and true, then it is not a fallacy.

A fine line divides a justified credibility attack from an *ad hominem* attack. In each case, whether evaluating opponents or the experts they cite, be sure to determine if the

credibility attack is relevant to the claim. If your opponent cites Joseph Stalin, the late
Soviet dictator, on the nature of his regime, obviously a statement about Stalin's character
would not be an *ad hominem* attack. Stalin killed millions of Soviet citizens in the guise of
political necessity, and his name has been all but erased from contemporary Soviet culture.
Any statement Stalin made about his regime must be considered in light of his character. A
good rule of thumb is to combine a credibility attack of another's sources with other
arguments as well. In that way, you can't be accused of *substituting* the person for the
argument.

FALLACY OF FALSE CONSOLATION

Many contemporary debate rounds boil down to which position has the the least
risk and the most benefits. **The fallacy of false consolation** takes that position to an
extreme by confusing a least harmful situation with a completely desirable situation. When
you console someone, you tell them that things are really O.K. When you falsely console
someone, you tell them things are O.K. when they really are not. Look at the example of a
false consolation fallacy:

I guess that I have no reason to complain. I mean I know my well has been
polluted with toxic waste and I'll probably die of cancer in 30 years. However, I
really don't have a problem compared to people in Africa that have no water at all
and will die of dehydration tomorrow.

The fact that toxic waste has contaminated this person's drinking water is a
problem. Just because people suffer greater harm elsewhere does not negate her problem.
She needs to confront her problem, and others in the world need to confront theirs. Merely
because some people are better off than others does not justify maintaining an undesirable
status quo.

THE FALSE DILEMMA FALLACY

The prefix "di" means "two." A true dilemma forces an advocate to make a choice
between two undesirable alternatives. A **false dilemma** attempts to force the same
choice; however, the difference is that, with the false dilemma there are actually more than
two options, and the additional options are desirable. When Reagan was accused in the
Iran-Contra affair, the media tried to put him into a true dilemma: Either Reagan did not
know what happened and he was incompetent, or he did know and he was corrupt. When
defending himself against the accusation, Reagan tried to prove that the dilemma actually
was false. Reagan suggested that his management style involved giving general directions
to subordinates then allowing them to carry out the specifics, which explains why he might
not have known what happened. Therefore, Reagan presented a third option not mentioned
by the media: He did not know what happened, but he was still a competent manager.
While there is still much doubt in many American's minds, Reagan's remark represents the
correct strategy to use when advocates are pinned to a dilemma.
The phrase, "America: tolerate it or leave it," is another example of a false dilemma.
There are other options besides the two undesirable ones listed. You could "change it" or
"love it," for instance. When forced into a dilemma, simply show the critic that there is a
desirable third or even fourth option not mentioned by your opponents. Thus, you prove
the dilemma false and escape losing the particular point.

THE FALLACY OF IGNORING THE ISSUE

Normally, the **fallacy of ignoring the issue** occurs in the cross examination period of a debate. If the respondents fail to answer directly the questions posed to them, they may be guilty of this fallacy. An occurrence of this fallacy may transpire as follows:

Questioner: Isn't it true that the McCabe study's conclusion contradicts your position here?

Respondent: We cite many other studies with the same inference.

Questioner: You mean you misrepresent many other studies, too?

Respondent: For instance, the Jones and Johnson study read in 1AC clearly demonstrates what we're trying to say.

Questioner: Look, I don't care about that. I want to know about the McCabe study you just read. Doesn't McCabe's conclusion contradict your position here?

Respondent: Will you let me answer the question my way. I need to explain the Jones and Johnson study.

Obviously, the respondent fails to address the question about the McCabe study. Instead of answering the question, the respondent ignores the issue and instead talks about another study altogether. If you find yourself in the position of the questioner, you need to make it clear in cross examination or in your team's next speech that the other team failed to answer that particular question. You are also free to speculate as to why the respondent failed to respond: Perhaps you were correct in observing that the McCabe study's conclusion contradicted the team's position.

THE FALLACY OF THE LOADED QUESTION

A **loaded question** assumes a premise that has yet to be established. If you answer a loaded question, you tacitly concede that the premise is true. "When did you stop sniffing glue?" is an example of a loaded question. That question assumes the premise that you once sniffed glue and that you have stopped. If you were to answer, "yesterday," you would be conceding to that premise.

When confronted with a loaded question, immediately point out that it is a loaded question, then address the premise, not the question. In answer to the "glue" question above, you should say (and hopefully with some degree of honesty), "that is a loaded question. I have never sniffed glue, and I don't appreciate the insinuation." Even asking the questioner to rephrase the question might be a good option to exercise. A loaded question, after all, is a thinly disguised accusation.

THE *AD POPULUM* FALLACY

Occasionally, the non-policy debate advocate will support a position with an opinion poll. If that is done to show how people feel about a particular issue, then that is a legitimate approach. However, if an opinion poll is used to support a particular position, then that may be an *ad populum* **fallacy**. *Ad populum* literally means "of the people." Just because people believe something to be true does not make it true. At one time, much of the world believed that the earth was flat. Obviously, people's beliefs did not make the earth flat. If your opponent argues that abortion is justified because the majority of Americans favor it, simply point out that your opponent is guilty of an *ad populum* fallacy.

Ultimately, democracy is founded upon this type of fallacy. Voting makes right whatever the majority feels is right. That is why it is not only important for us to vote, but it is also important for us to make an informed choice when we do so. Democracy's success depends upon having a knowledgeable voting public. Additionally, the popular opinion has sometimes stood against what in retrospect many of us view as truth. Socrates, Christ, Copernicus, Galileo, Thoreau, Freud, M.L. King, Jr., and others suffered unjust criticism because they espoused beliefs that differed from the popular opinion of their time.

THE FALLACY OF PSYCHOLOGICAL LANGUAGE

A technique enjoyed by numerous novice debaters is the fallacy of psychological language. This fallacy includes both baiting an opponent and using loaded language. **Baiting an opponent** involves insulting an opponent or rudely criticizing an opponent's argument. Whereas the *ad hominem* fallacy concerns attacking a person's character, baiting an opponent simply means attempting to anger the other person. This fallacy usually assumes that the instigator of the baiting does so consciously. However, more often than not, the novice debater does it unknowingly. After a debate round, someone might mention to the debater that he or she was rude, and that debater may not have realized it. If an opponent angers you, you must try to keep your cool. There is little worse for a critic than watching two novice debaters verbally assault one another.

The fallacy of loaded language involves using emotionally laden words rather than sound logic. Someone may argue that "the evil and tyrannous Democratic Party should be curtailed from its dictatorial operations in the U.S. congress before the world explodes into nuclear holocaust and kills all of the angelic Republicans." This argument has not a shred of proof in it, yet it seems rather compelling. After all, who is going to argue against angels and in support of evil and tyrannous dictators? When confronted with an opponent who tends to sound good, but lacks evidence, be sure to mention the lack of proof to the critic.

THE FALLACY OF THE STRAW PERSON

The **fallacy of the straw person** involves ignoring the real issue and arguing a similar but less threatening issue instead. The metaphor, *straw person*, refers to a physical fight in which a person decides to wrestle the easy-to-beat straw person rather than the tough-to-beat real person. In a debate on air pollution, you might argue that diesel engines pose a great health risk. Your opponent, lacking evidence on diesel exhaust, might respond with evidence proving that smog devices on gasoline engines work well. While gasoline engines pose a similar pollution problem as do diesel engines, gasoline engines are only tangentially relevant. Therefore, you would need to point out that your opponent has committed a straw argument and explain that your original argument about diesel effects still stands.

THE FALLACY OF TRADITION

The fallacy of tradition occurs when someone equates the best way to do something with the way it traditionally has been done. An opponent may argue, "For nearly a century the U.S. government has generated revenue through income taxes, so that must be the best way to finance national expenditures." However, just because it has been done that way does not make it the best way. If you hear such a fallacy of tradition, you need to explain that your opponent committed the fallacy and that the issue in question thus remains unsupported.

NON SEQUITUR

Non sequitur literally means, "it does not follow." This fallacy occurs when a conclusion does not follow from the premises or the evidence. For instance, someone might argue, "He must be a moral man; he has nice clothes." This is a non sequitur because being moral does not follow from having nice clothes.

SUMMARY

In this chapter, some of the more common fallacies were discussed. In order to become proficient at identifying fallacies, however, you need to do more than merely read a chapter explaining fallacies. You really need to make identification of fallacies an ongoing effort. Some texts even suggest trying to identify at least one fallacy a day. Advertisements, newspaper articles, network news broadcasts, classroom lectures, interpersonal conversations, books, letters, group discussions, speeches, debates, *etc.* are good sources of fallacies. Critical thinking is something that requires more than mere knowledge acquisition. You need to make critical thinking a habit or even a philosophy by which to live.

7| POLICY VS. QUASI-POLICY

A look at CEDA resolutions over the years suggests that many topics have been quasi-policy in nature. An example of a quasi-policy topic is "Resolved: That implementing the military draft in the United States would be desirable." In Chapter One of this text, a quasi-policy topic was defined as a topic which evaluates a suggested policy change. At this writing there is no military draft, so the above topic is a quasi-policy topic because it is evaluating (determining the desirability of) a suggested policy of military draft. What quasi-policy debating has come to mean in academia is debating a policy without debating the mechanics of a concrete plan. In other words, the affirmative still has the burden to prove the merits of a structural change in the *status quo*, but the affirmative does not have the requirement to discuss the specific means by which that change will be achieved. However, that is a simplified explanation. Really, nothing in the policy debating realm, including the plan, is prohibited when debating quasi-policy topics. The difference is more a matter of format, and less a matter of content.

A policy debate traditionally follows the justification-and-plan format discussed in Chapter One. A quasi-policy debate normally follows the definitive-and designative format discussed throughout this text. While the format differs significantly, the content does not differ substantially. A quasi-policy debater may discuss policy stock issues, but must do so within the non-policy format. The policy debater may wish to discuss values or criterion-satisfaction, but usually does so within the policy format. The rest of this chapter is devoted to helping the beginner approach quasi-policy and even policy topics.

TRADITIONAL POLICY STOCK ISSUES

When debating quasi-policy topics, most critics still expect affirmative advocates to follow the definitive-designative format. However, an understanding of policy debating can enhance an advocate's argumentation on quasi-policy topics. Of special interest to quasi-policy debaters is a discussion of the policy stock issues.

In Chapter One, justification and plan stock issues for policy debate were discussed. For further explication of the policy stock issues, a **medical analogy** can be helpful. The analogy is slightly different from the model discussed in Chapter One.

However, it includes all of the same elements, just by different names; those new names include **Ill, Blame Cure, and Cost**. *Ill* refers to significant harm. In order for a society to justify change there has to be a significant reason for change. Our major institutions do not make major changes in policy without a serious and compelling reason.

Ill

The medical analogy suggests that you do not have major surgery unless your life is threatened (significant harm). In the same way our institutions should not make major policy changes unless justified. If a negative advocate were able to prove that there is no harm or that the harm is insignificant, the negative should win the debate. The affirmative must win all of the stock issues in order to win a debate; the negative only need win one. Back to the medical analogy, should a second opinion prove to you that your life is not threatened, you may decide against a surgical procedure.

Blame

Blame refers to inherency, the reason that the problem exists. A discussion of blame assumes that if the *status quo* is not inherently flawed there is then no reason for major changes. The affirmative in a policy debate is required to show that the *status quo* is structurally flawed, thus justifying a major change of policy. The medical analogy suggests that something serious must have caused an illness, thus requiring major corrective medical procedures. For example, if you had serious kidney problems, such that regular dialysis was barely keeping you alive, the doctor would probably recommend a kidney transplant. In other words, your physiological condition was inherently flawed and needed major corrective surgery. On the other hand, what if you were merely feverish and felt some pain? Although this may require remedy, it is not a condition requiring major surgery. You may just have a small kidney stone that can pass with minor medical treatment. The difference between minor treatment and major surgery is the difference between the negative and the affirmative respectively in a policy debate. The affirmative must opt for the major surgery and must prove that the organs are inherently flawed. However, if the negative can prove that the condition is minor, the negative should win the debate. This negative strategy is called a **minor repair**. If the negative successfully advances a minor repair, there should be no need for the overly corrective affirmative resolution. The successful implementation of a minor repair should result in a negative ballot.

Let's expand upon this other analogy, minor repair. You're trying to decide what to do about your car. It does not run. You ask yourself, "do I need a new engine?" The implied resolution is "Resolved: That I should get a new engine for my car." In order for you to adopt the resolution, you will need to prove to yourself that the major, costly repair is justified. If you have cracked the engine's block, thrown a rod, and frozen your engine from running it with no oil, your engine would have the structural flaws needed to justify getting a new one. The current engine is useless. No mechanic in town could repair a cracked block. The affirmative would win the inherency issue; the engine is inherently and structurally flawed. If on the other hand you could convince yourself that your car just needs a new set of spark plugs (a minor repair), then there would be no need to get a new engine or adopt the resolution. The negative would win the inherency issue and the debate. Remember, the affirmative must win all of the stock issues; the negative only need win one.

Cure

In addition to the concept of inherency or blame, an advocate also must consider the stock issue of cure. Cure involves offering a plan; a **plan** is a concrete course of action. Normally, a plan includes references to the following: agency, mandates, enforcement, and funding. Other items may be included in a plan such as promulgation and exemptions, but these four elements are the minimum necessary. Table 14 shows an example of a basic plan. Affirmative advocates may create virtually any plan that they see fit.

The reason that the affirmative has such latitude is due to academic debate's notion of fiat. Fiat in this context is not a small car that breaks down all the time. Rather, **fiat** is the power to put something hypothetically into existence for the purposes of debating its worth. In other words, the debater does not have to prove that something will happen, only that something should happen. Fiat power precludes the policy debater from having to prove that congress and the president will support the affirmative plan. Fiat power makes the pragmatics of politics as such irrelevant to the academic debate. The debaters and the judge take on governmental power to implement whichever plan they see fit. The focus of the debate should be on the merits of a given plan, not on whether some brain-dead politician will vote for it. You may fiat the existence of a new administrating body, a new law, a new penalty, a new branch of the military, or a new branch of the government. You must still prove the worth of those items, but you need not prove that the items will become part of the *status quo*. There are however limitations to fiat power. You may not fiat an attitude change, and you may not fiat impossible technologies. For example, you may not fiat into existence a device which will render all radioactive materials inert. Fiat power is limited to the political nature of policy adoption. Fiat power simply allows the debaters to become legislators for the day. Whatever is within the power of the government is also within the purview of the debate round. Fiat power, however, does not include the ability to go beyond present human capabilities.

While advocates have the advantage of fiat, affirmative advocates must provide a topical and a workable plan. To be topical, the plan must stick to the words of the resolution. Think of the resolution as a playing field. If you go outside the boundaries of the field your play does not count. If you stay within the field, then you may win or score a point. The same is true with debating. If you stay within the topic, only then may you win. Going outside of the topic may not only cause your plan not to count, but it also may result in your losing the debate altogether. Let's consider the topic, "Resolved: That the U.S. Government should provide economic aid to non-democratic nations." If an affirmative team offered a plan for Canada to give military aid to a democracy, the affirmative team would be nontopical on three points. The affirmative team would be nontopical because, first, the resolution said *U.S.*, not *Canada*; second, the resolution said *economic*, not *military* aid; and third, the resolution said *non-democratic nation*, not *democracy*. If the negative team clearly issued a topicality argument, the affirmative should lose the debate. (See Chapter Three for a more involved explanation of Topicality.)

Besides being topical, the affirmative plan must also be workable. Workability means that the technical aspects of the plan must be able to operate as intended, without any glitches. The plan in Table 14 may fall victim to a negative workability argument. The enforcement section mentions criminal prosecution. The negative could argue that most lumber companies are corporations. The negative also might be able to find evidence that says that it is nearly impossible to apply a criminal prosecution to a corporation. If that were so, the affirmative plan may be unenforceable, thus unworkable.

As in all stock issues, the negative only need neutralize one to win the debate. If the negative wins either the topicality or workability argument, the negative should win the debate. The affirmative must win this and all other stock issues. Recall the medical analogy; if a patient were given an appendectomy for cancer of the larynx, that would certainly not help the cancerous condition. The cancerous larynx would still be in the body. The operation to remove the appendix would be unhelpful and, in debate terms, unworkable and nontopical.

TABLE 14
Policy Debate's Version of a Plan

Plank One: Agency: The Department of the Interior will oversee the project.   The department will create an agency to insure the mandates are carried out.   The agency will be entitled The Old-Growth Preservation Commission.

Plank Two: Mandates: A. The states will set aside all old growth timber.   B. All old-growth timber harvesting will be prohibited.   C. The federal government will supply lumber corporations with subsidies for the set-aside land. The subsidy program will be similar to the farm subsidy program, but the payments will take place over a twenty-year period.

Plank Three: Enforcement: A. Under this plan, harvesting of old growth timber will be felonious. Criminal prosecution will result in the minimum sentence of 6 months in jail and a $10,000.00 fine.   B. States that fail to comply with the mandates may lose eligibility in any of a number of federally-funded programs.

Plank Four: Funding: Funding will come from federal and state general revenues.

Plank Five: Addenda: Exemptions will include the following: A. Removal of trees when necessary for fire protection or control. B. Removal of trees as a part of general forest management.   C. Applications for other exemptions may be filed with the commission for review. All exemptions must entail a compelling state interest.

Cost

Cost is the final stock issue. It obviously refers to the costs accrued from implementing a plan, but it also refers to advantages and benefits. In medical terms, if you were to have costly plastic surgery that would deplete life savings and have little chance of adding anything to your quality of life, you probably would not have the surgery. The cost in this case outweighs the benefits.

This stock issue is also referred to as **advantage**. What advantages or disadvantages will result from plan implementation? The affirmative debaters themselves are not required to list the disadvantages; however, when the negative argues disadvantages (disads), the affirmative must be able to prove that the advantages from the plan outweigh the disadvantages.

A second important element is that of solvency. **Solvency** is the requirement to prove that the affirmative plan can correct the current harms. Solvency can also be quantified. For instance, say an affirmative team were to argue that the U.S. should fund family counseling programs for domestic violence cases. And say the affirmative were able to locate evidence that indicates that in 80 to 90 percent of the cases, counseling prevents further abuse. The 80-to-90-percent evidence thus provides the quantification for the solvency requirement. Eight out of ten violent family members never resort to violence again. Through implementation of the plan, the affirmative would prove that a significant part of the problem could be solved. Of course, much of the domestic violence will continue. It is not the job of the affirmative to prove one-hundred percent solvency. The affirmative need only prove that a significant part of the problem will be corrected.

Sometimes it is not possible to provide quantification. In that case, testimony evidence, cause-effect evidence, or even analogy evidence can help to prove solvency. An affirmative advocate might be able to locate a quotation from an expert that attests to the validity of a similar plan. Similarly, one might be able to find cause-effect evidence. The cause would be your plan; the effect would be the correction of ills. Finally, analogy evidence is a great way to provide solvency. If you could prove that somewhere else in the world a similar plan solved related problems, you could go a long way toward proving your plan solvent.

Understanding the traditional policy stock issues is helpful; however, they are only one of the many ways to approach policy topics.

COMPARATIVE-ADVANTAGE POLICY STOCK ISSUES

The comparative-advantage approach is another way to address a policy topic. Simply, the comparative-advantage case concedes that there may be no harm in the *status quo*. Instead, the affirmative argues that the *status quo* could be improved; in other words, the world could be made comparatively better through implementation of the affirmative plan. The traditional stock issues of ill, blame, cure and cost move the world from a harmful place to a harmless place. The comparative-advantage stock issues move the world from an inert, advantage-less world, to a beautiful, advantageous world. Table 15 shows a continuum with harm at one end and advantages at the other. A traditional case eliminates a harmful condition to reach a harmless or slightly advantageous position on the continuum. A comparative advantage case starts at the harmless part of the continuum and moves society to an extremely advantageous position. In a comparative-advantage affirmative case, the blame and cure stock issues remain basically the same. Instead of addressing the ill stock issue, however, the comparative-advantage affirmative team simply shows that the desired advantages do not now exist. The cost stock issue also is slightly different in that it explores a comparison between present advantages and the affirmative plan's advantages. These concepts are discussed further throughout the rest of this chapter.

Now that the policy stock issues have been reviewed, it is important to look at the implications of policy theory for quasi-policy topics. A discussion of **Operational Definitions as Plan, Criteria and the Solvency Requirement, Justification in Quasi-Policy Debating, Inherency and Minor Repair**, and **Counterplan** should give the advocate a clearer understanding of how policy theory applies to non-policy debating.

TABLE 15
Harm-Advantage Continuum

<u>Harmful</u>   <u>Harmless</u>   <u>Advantageous</u>

x   >   x   x   >   x
        Traditional Policy Case   Comparative Advantage

OPERATIONAL DEFINITIONS AS PLAN

People associated with academic debate tend to classify quasi-policy topics as policy topics without the requirement for a plan. However, CEDA participants have resorted to outright plans when necessary to clarify an affirmative position. The suggestion offered here is to incorporate the notion of plan in the definitions of the policy terms of the resolution. For instance, a quasi-policy topic which reads, "Resolved: That increased training for teachers in the United States would be desirable," offers a policy phrase requiring explanation. The phrase, "increased training for teachers," would not be well explained with simple dictionary definitions; although, that's a good place to start. Really, in order to debate this topic, the affirmative would need to give the critic some idea of what type of training it advocates. After defining terms using dictionary definitions, perhaps the affirmative could include a statement at the end of the definition section which said something such as the following: "We operationally define increased training for teachers to mean twenty hours per year of additional instruction in drug counseling." Such an explanation would help to clarify the affirmative position and to limit the debate: both of which are beneficial to the affirmative.

However, if you do choose to use operational definitions, realize that you must adhere to those definitions throughout the debate. What that means is that all of your evidence should refer specifically to whatever definition you offered. If you gave an operational definition which said <u>increased instruction in drug counseling</u>, you won't be able to claim an advantage from some other form of training. While operational definitions can serve the function of a plan, be careful not to define yourself out of the debate.

Depending on your critic or instructor, you may be able to offer even a more involved plan such as the one listed in Table 14. However, since many critics see the absence of a plan as the last stand for non-policy debate, you should be careful in front of which critic you debate such a plan. Realize, too, that if you offer a plan, be careful that your plan is both workable and topical.

CRITERIA AND THE SOLVENCY REQUIREMENT

Solvency can be an important concern when an advocate is faced with a quasi-policy topic. In order to prove the desirability of a policy change, the affirmative may need to prove that the new policy will correct any harm in the *status quo*. The affirmative criterion often serves as the focal point of the solvency concern.

Let's look at the quasi-policy topic, "Resolved: That increased oil drilling off of the U.S. coastlines would be desirable." For that topic, an affirmative team might offer the criterion of economic security. Later in the case, the affirmative advocates might argue that the economy could not stomach an oil crisis, and that an oil crisis would tip the economy into a recession. With those serious risks recorded, the affirmative advocates would have to prove that their resolution serves as the solution to those potential ills. In other words, the affirmative would have to provide solvency evidence. Perhaps evidence could be found to indicate that increased drilling could provide enough low cost petroleum to offset the effects of an oil crisis. Unfortunately, that solvency evidence may not exist, thus leaving the affirmative with no warrant for the resolution. More than likely, the negative in such a debate could press the solvency issue and provide evidence that suggests that an aggressive drilling program wouldn't help even in a moderate oil crunch. The impact to the negative's argument, of course, is that the affirmative team has not met its burden to prove solvency. That burden stemmed from the affirmative criterion of economic security.

JUSTIFICATION IN QUASI-POLICY DEBATING

Qualitative and Quantitative Harm

In order to justify a quasi-policy resolution, an affirmative advocate must show some justifiable need for the suggested change. That justification may come in the form of significant harm (ill). And advocates may demonstrate that significant harm in two ways: through qualitative significance and/or through quantitative significance.

Qualitative significance refers to the erosion of significant human values such as freedom or equality. Think of the root word in qualitative: quality. When the quality of life is adversely affected then that is a qualitative harm. For example, perhaps not may Americans die from terrorist attacks; however, many Americans do not feel free to travel to some parts of the world. The lack of freedom is significant qualitatively; our quality of life is affected adversely by international terrorism.

Whereas qualitative significance refers to the harm to our value system, quantitative significance refers to quantity or numbers. Again, think of the root word here: quantity. Usually, quantitative significance looks for the amount of financial loss, human injury, and human death.

Let's look at the quasi-policy topic, "Resolved: That increasing the number of shelters for victims of domestic violence would be desirable." In order to help justify that topic you would have to prove that domestic violence is significant enough to demand an increased number of shelters. If you could show that 50 million people are seriously injured and thousands are killed during incidents of domestic violence, you would go a long way toward proving significance. Of course, since the topic refers to "increasing the number of shelters," among other things, you also would have to prove that there is not nearly enough shelter space to fill the need. You might also have to prove that, because there is inadequate shelter space, a significant number of family members are forced to remain in a dangerous environment. Furthermore, you would have to show causality in terms of the number of family members that suffer worse fates because of the lack of refuge. The bottom line is that your critic needs to know that additional shelter space is needed.

Qualitative and quantitative justification may be used separately or together. Qualitative alone, however, is sometimes looked upon as a weak justification. You may need to justify to your critic the sole use of qualitative significance. Quantitative harm alone is hardly ever a problem. The best approach, of course, is to use both qualitative and quantitative.

Let's look at the quasi-policy topic, "Resolved: That banning practices which are harmful to the ozone layer would be desirable." An affirmative advocate could argue the quantitative harm of the number of injurious and fatal skin cancer cases due to increased ozone depletion. The Environmental Protection Agency (EPA) estimates that a one percent drop in ozone causes an additional 43,000 cases of skin cancer annually in the United States. EPA's worst case scenario involves an additional 261 million skin cancer cases and 5.6 million cancer deaths during the next 80 years. Darrel Rigel, Associate Professor of Dermatology at the New York University, says "that would mean that virtually everyone in the country would get skin cancer. And it wouldn't be from lying out in the sun. The radiation would be so intense it wouldn't take much more than walking around in the street." Obviously, the figures from the EPA and the interpretation of those figures by Rigel paint a pretty ominous picture of the quantitative effects of ozone depletion. An advocate using these statistics would prove easily that something needs to be done. Additionally, an affirmative advocate also could argue the qualitative results of ozone depletion: People would not be as free to spend as much time out of doors. Among other things the freedom to enjoy nature would be impeded.

Comparative-Advantage Justification

One way to help justify a quasi-policy topic is to provide quantitative and qualitative significance. Another way to justify a topic is to argue a comparative advantage. If you were to approach the quasi-policy topic, "Resolved: That a significant increase in special education in the United States would be desirable," a comparative advantage approach might be appropriate. A topic such as this may not lend itself to the ill-blame-cure-cost model because there may be no significant harm in the *status quo*. Perhaps special education students are being helped in a minimal fashion, with little or no resultant harm. Instead of arguing harm or ill, you could argue the criterion of employability or mainstreaming. In the application of that criterion, you could argue that, although students are being helped, they are not being helped to excel. You might argue further that, with the right training (that would entail a significant increase in special education in the United States), a fairly significant percentage of special education students could find productive employment in mainstream USA. Thus, you would fulfill your criterion and in the process develop a strong argument for increased special education. And you did that without ever arguing a single instance of harm.

INHERENCY AND MINOR REPAIR

In order to justify the policy change suggested by your topic, the affirmative advocate may need to show that the harm is inherent in the *status quo*. One way to prove the inherency issue is by showing that one of the major institutions is structurally flawed. In other words, an affirmative advocate could prove that one of the major institutions is a significant contributor to the cause of the harmful situation. There are eight major institutions common to all societies throughout humanity's history: family, religion, military, education, medicine, law, government, and economy. Any one of these could be contributing to the harmful situation. Additionally, many other modern institutions have also found their way into our world. These could also contribute to the problem:

transportation, mass media, the arts, *etc.* Subgroups within the major institutions may also help cause the problem.

Taking an in-depth look at institutional framework can give you a good start into proving the inherency issue. For instance, on the nuclear freeze topic, an affirmative team may want to focus on the military establishment. Perhaps the military is inherently flawed because it wants to build weapons no matter what the foreign-affairs climate. The military may also be flawed because it doesn't train its strategists in the dogma of diplomacy. Consequently, the military mind will not accept a freeze. It would not do so because it would be cutting its own throat if it did. When the make up of an institution contributes to the problem, it is called **structural inherency**.

Attitudinal inherency, on the other hand, refers to the way in which people's attitudes and beliefs contribute to a problem. For instance, women in this country still suffer from discrimination. This harmful situation is perpetrated by antiquated beliefs and attitudes about women's place in society. Persistence of such attitudes contributes to the on-going problem. One of the arguments for the Equal Rights Amendment was that it would have provided the legal remedy needed for a belief system that precludes equality.

Through structural or attitudinal inherency or both, the affirmative advocate can build a strong inherency argument. However, the negative is not without armour to defense the inherency attack. First, the negative can argue causality. Previous chapters covered how to argue causality. Basically, the negative advocate must show that the attitudinal or structural causes are not sufficient in strength to produce the asserted effect. Second, the negative could deny causality. In other words, the negative could simply press or provide evidence that the inherent situation does not exist at all. A third option is to argue minor repair.

When arguing a minor repair, a negative advocate need not give up the *status quo*. Basically, what the negative must argue is that the *status quo* can be repaired with just a slight adjustment. In other words, the *status quo* is still viable and is not in need of significant correction. If the negative team manages to win the minor repair, the negative should win the debate. On the gun control topic, affirmative teams attempted to prove that *status quo* was dangerously flawed. They argued that thousands of people needlessly die from accidents and crimes. A lack of tough legislation and a misinterpretation of the U.S. Constitution contributed to much of the problem, or so the affirmative arguments went. On the surface, the harms seemed inherent.

However, many negative teams countered with a minor repair of education and enforcement. The negative advocates argued that gun control was not needed. They argued that education would prevent accidents, and they argued that vigorous enforcement of existing laws would keep convicted criminals from getting guns. Education, in this context, was a minor repair because it did not substantially alter the structure of existing institutions. An educational campaign would merely inform people how to use a gun. Enforcement of existing laws was a minor repair because it also did not significantly change the status quo. In fact, enforcement was actually an endorsement of the *status quo*; what enforcement did, according to the negative advocates, was make the *status quo* regulations work.

The affirmative team must endorse the creation of new laws or some significant equivalent. For that reason, endorsement of existing laws is not affirmative ground. Therefore, a minor repair is always a justified response on a quasi-policy resolution.

COUNTERPLAN

The only time that a counterplan should be run by the negative is when debating quasi-policy topics. Counterplans must be non-topical and competitive. When presenting a counterplan the negative must make sure that its proposal is *not* topical. If it were topical, the affirmative could claim it as their own. Additionally, it has to be competitive with the affirmative proposal. One test for competitiveness is whether the counterplan is mutually exclusive with the affirmative's suggested policy. In other words, the affirmative cannot have its suggested policy and the negative's counterplan as well. Competitiveness also means that the negative proposal must be *better* than the affirmative's. For example, during the unilateral freeze topic, affirmatives were asked to prove the quasi-policy concept that a unilateral freeze would be desirable. Negatives quickly realized that a unilateral freeze may not be the best alternative when dealing with the nuclear problem. Therefore, some negatives offered an alternative counterplan of a bilateral freeze. This approach is quite effective most of the time on quasi-policy topics. When arguing a counterplan, realize that the negative surrenders presumption and gives up the *status quo*. Basically, the negative is saying, "We agree that there is a problem, but we feel that there is a better solution than those provided for by the resolution and the affirmative team." Counterplans are run in 1NC.

POLICY DEBATING

Nothing in the CEDA Constitution precludes the use of policy topics. In fact, policy topics have been considered by the membership each semester for the past few years. Even Ronald Matlon, the person who wrote one of the original theoretical explanations of value debate, argues in the 1988 issue of the *CEDA Yearbook* that academia should return to policy debate. Some scholars even argue that non-policy debate never really existed. This chapter gives some credence to that notion; although, that certainly was not the intention.

A CEDA return to policy debating should not confound coaches or debaters. Policy debating has a much more developed, much more concrete theoretical base. And there are many unique benefits to debating policy topics. Of course, there are controversies within that theory as there are with any others, and this author would prefer the Cross Examination Debate Association retain the non-policy version of its topics. However, CEDA may very well move back into the policy realm.

Affirmative advocates in a policy debate must present a *prima-facie* case in the first affirmative speech. The case must include reference to the ill, blame, cure, and cost. An outline of a brainstormed policy case can be seen in Table 16. Once the brainstorming is done, debaters would need to research each point to see whether there exists any evidence of support. Each of the sub-points in the first, second, and fourth contention would require documentation. The third major argument, the plan, may or may not be evidenced. Because the affirmative has fiat power, the plan need not be documented. Notice how each major argument in Table 16 concerns itself with a stock issue. Contention one deals with the ill stock issue. Contention two addresses blame or inherency. The third major argument involves an explanation of the affirmative's plan (cure). And the fourth major argument addresses the cost stock issue: solvency, advantages vs. disadvantages.

Another option for debating policy debate is to argue a **comparative advantage case**, which uses the following structure: first, show that the advantages do not now exist; second, show that the status quo is inherently incapable of achieving the desired advantages; third, offer a plan; and fourth, show that your plan will result in the comparative advantages. To organize such a case, you would follow a similar format as found in Table 16. However, instead of a contention one dealing with harm, you would develop a contention explaining that the desired advantages do not now exist. The second contention would still concern itself with inherency, but it is inherency of a slightly different kind. This type of inherency deals primarily with proving that the status quo is inherently incapable of producing such desirable effects. The third major argument, the plan, follows the same format as do all plans. And finally, the fourth major argument, cost, is also the same as the traditional case, except there is usually no reference to solvency. You simply list the comparative advantages.

TABLE 16
Brainstormed Policy Debate Outline

Resolved: That the federal government should significantly increase its commitment to education.

I. Poor education causes economic and social problems (ill).
    A. Schools are not retaining students.
        1. Adolescents who drop out early become a burden on society at a significant cost annually (quantitative harm).
        2. Adolescents who drop out early are more likely to become involved in criminal behavior.
        3. Crime by dropouts results in significant harm (monetary loss, injury, and murder) to other members of society (quantitative harm).

    B. Schools are not training the needed work force.
        1. Increased vocational training is needed to keep our economy afloat.
        2. The lack of vocational training may be a key contributing factor to a future recession.
        3. Quality of life will be adversely affected in a recession. (qualitative harm)

II. The problem is inherent (blame).
    A. Schools are not equipped to retain students.
        1. There are inadequate resources to retain students (structural)
        2. School personnel do not care about the dropout problem (attitudinal).

    B. Schools are not equipped to offer vocational education.
        1. By the end of the next two decades, 80 percent of the jobs will require at least two years of advanced training.
        2. Schools simply are not prepared to handle the sheer numbers of people who will require vocational training (structural).

III. Plan (Cure).
    Plank One: Agency: The program will be run through the Dept. of Education.
                    A Retention and Voc. Ed. Commission will be established.
    Plank Two: Mandates: The program will mandate retention and vocational educational programs for K-14. Goals will be established as follows: one, half of those now dropping out will be retained; two, the number of students currently in vocational programs will be doubled.
    Plank Three: Enforcement: Schools who fail to reach established goals may be denied further funding.
    Plank Four: Funding: The program will be funded by a national lottery.

IV. Advantages (Cost).
    A. Higher retention of students reduces crime (solvency).
    B. More vocational education will enhance the economy (advantage).

The goals case is a third option in arguing a policy resolution. The goals case is very similar to the definitions-criteria-application format of non-policy debate. In fact, the goals case is also called the criterion-satisfaction case. Usually, this type of case follows a four step process similar to the comparative advantage. The first step of the goals case is to outline a goal of the status quo. To do that, you could quote a governmental official, such as the current U.S. President. Perhaps the President has set goals for an area of your topic in which you have an interest. You would need to locate an official government document outlining that goal, or you could find a goal statement issued by the President or the White-House staff. Additional data in contention one could support the worth of such a goal. Perhaps the goal is to land a human on the planet, Mars. Along with the official or semi-official acknowledgement of such a goal, you would need to prove to your critic why such a space mission is needed. In the second contention, you must show why the goal cannot now be achieved. Again, this is inherency in a slightly different form; you argue that the *status quo* is incapable of achieving the stated goal. The third major argument is, as usual, the plan. The fourth major argument lists the key advantages from adopting the plan and fulfilling the goal.

Alternative justification is another variation of a policy case. Alternative justification involves the affirmative offering more than one case. The theory is that if the affirmative wins but one of the cases, the affirmative should win the debate. This is different from the stock issue analysis discussed at the beginning of this chapter. Essentially, if the affirmative wins one of its cases, it has won all of the stock issues; albeit, only one complete version. The affirmative may also offer alternative plans for a single case. In other words, major arguments one (ill), two (blame), and four (advantage) would remain the same. Alternative plans would be offered to compliment the case. The same theory holds true for the alternative plans. The affirmative only needs to justify one of the plans to win the debate.

First negatives in a policy debate traditionally refute the ill, blame, and cost stock issues using four-point refutation. And just as in non-policy debating, first negatives must address all operational issues, such as topicality, minor repairs, and counterplans. In fact, in competitive policy debating, many first negatives simply offer a counterplan and concede ill and blame. Second negatives in a policy debate are responsible for neutralizing the affirmative plan. To do that, second negatives offer disadvantages to the plan. Disads are structured just like value objections, and show what bad things would happen if the affirmative plan were adopted. Second negatives also issue workability arguments.

SUMMARY

This chapter discussed the relevance of policy debating to quasi-policy debating. The latter is really a hybrid of two forms of debating: Quasi-policy debating borrows nearly every principle both from the value and from the policy realms. Advocates should feel free to find whatever they need in either camp. As mentioned, however, some critics do not allow quasi-policy debates to become entrenched in plan arguments, so be sure to consult carefully with your argumentation instructor or your debate coach before constructing a complex plan. And should CEDA vote in a policy topic, this chapter also gave you some practical advice for approaching policy topics.

APPENDIX A
AFFIRMATIVE CASE

Erwin Knoll, in *The Minnesota Law Review*, 1982, writes,

Whenever anyone finds it necessary or expedient to weigh freedom in the balance against any other consideration, freedom is likely to be found wanting. That certainly is the case when freedom of speech and press is balanced against considerations of national security. The logic is irresistible: who would not gladly permit a trivial and temporary incursion against the Bill of Rights when the alternative might be military defeat or even a nuclear holocaust? That was precisely the logic Judge Warren articulated in the PROGRESSIVE CASE when he stated, "you can't speak freely when you're dead."

I find it extremely easy, therefore, to support the resolution: "Resolved: That significant government restrictions on coverage by the United States media of terrorist activity are justified."

OBSERVATION I We offer the following definitions:

Terrorism: The United Nations General Assembly in a resolution against terrorism, November 19, 1985, define terrorism as "acts . . . in all its forms which endanger or take innocent lives, jeopardize fundamental freedoms and seriously impair the dignity of human beings."

Significant: As defined by the *American Heritage Dictionary of the English Language*, 1981, means "important, notable, or valuable."

Government: From the *Random House Dictionary*, 1980, is defined as the political direction and control exercised over a nation, state, community, *etc*. . ."

Justified: from the *American Heritage Dictionary of the English Language*, 1981, is defined as "to demonstrate or prove to be just, right, or valid."

Is. as defined by *Blacks Law Dictionary*, 1968, "This word, although normally referring to the present, often has a future meaning, but is not synonymous with 'shall have been.' It may have, however, a past signification, as in the sense of 'has been.'"

Restrictions:. From the *Oxford American Dictionary*, "The act of limiting."

OBSERVATION II The criteria. Our criteria for judging this round is the legal standard of clear and present danger. Whenever there is a threat to the lives or safety of American citizens, that is a clear and present danger. In such a case, the government is, and always has been, justified in restricting the media. In Schenck vs. U.S. (268 U.S. 673), Justice Holmes, giving the opinion for the Supreme Court, writes,

> The question in every case is whether the words are used in such circumstances and are of such nature as to create a clear and present danger that they will bring about the substantive evils that the state has a right to protect.

CONTENTION I The Clear and Present Danger doctrine applies today.

Sub-point A. The first amendment protections of speech and press are not absolute. M. Cherif Bassiouni, professor of law at De Paul, in *The Journal of Criminal Law and Criminology*, 1981, states

> "The formulation of first amendment jurisprudence by the United States Supreme Court began with a series of cases involving subversive advocacy during WWI. In Schneck vs. U.S., Justice Holmes, writing for a unanimous Court, made it clear that protection afforded speech is not absolute but 'depends upon the circumstances in which it is done.'"

As Bassiouni indicates in her interpretation of the Holmes opinion, the first amendment does not guarantee speech at all costs. There are exceptions to the rule.

Sub-point B. One of the exceptions is media coverage of terrorism. Bassiouni, cited earlier, states in 1981, that,

> "The (clear and present danger) doctrine would appear to provide a basis for regulating media reporting of terrorist incidents in at least three instances: first, where the terrorist attacks are perceived as a 'demonstrated risk of specific threats to the social order'; second, in those rare circumstances where a media representative's remark could be construed as an incitement to lawless action; and third, where media dissemination of specific information immediately jeopardized the lives of hostages."

Here, Bassiouni clearly demonstrates the link between the clear and present danger doctrine and restricting media coverage of terrorism. Bassiouni indicates that media coverage must be regulated to guarantee the safety of any hostages and to protect the U.S. government. Therefore, even though the Supreme Court has yet to rule on media coverage of terrorism, a credible law professor tells us that the Court would clearly rule for restriction of media coverage of terrorism if given the opportunity. In fact,

Sub-point C. The Court has authorized many similar exceptions already, such as not being able to yell "fire" in a theater and not being able to publish subversive material. Bassiouni continues, "Even within the ambit of protected speech, the Supreme Court has recognized exceptions (under) the clear and present danger doctrine." Clearly, the first amendment is no longer an issue in this debate. We can still have operable speech and press protections, while restricting the media when they can endanger lives.

Contention II Terrorism presents a clear and present danger to U.S. citizens.

Sub-point A. U.S. citizens are an attractive target to terrorists. According to the *U.S. News and World Report* in 1985, "the (American death) toll (from terrorism) rises higher--yet at least 320 Americans have been murdered by terrorist since the 1980's began." One reason for this inexcusably high death rate is found in

Sub-point B. Terrorists favor the western world over the eastern world. Bassiouni, from De Paul, cited earlier, states, "The most active arenas for terrorist operations remained the industrial democracies of North America and Western Europe and the politically tense atmosphere of Latin America and the Middle East. These regions were the scene of over ninety percent of all terrorist incidents in the decade spanning 1968 to 1978." Even more frightening

Sub-point C. The U.S. itself is an attractive target. *The U.S. News and World Report*, July 8, 1985, reports,

> Another source of concern among anti-terrorist experts is the danger that Marxist terrorists from Central America might slip across the country's relatively open southern border with Mexico as easily as have hundreds of thousands of illegal aliens. 'I am not an alarmist,' says Dalager of Texas A&M University, 'But the building blocks are coming our way. It is just a matter of time.'

Clearly, U.S. citizens and the U.S. government are two of the more attractive terrorist targets. Media restrictions seem a logical protection to prevent unnecessary violence.

Contention III The media is feckless.

Sub-point A. Media gives away important information. Michael Elkins, consultant for *Newsweek* and vice-chair of the Foreign Press Association in Israel, *International Terrorism*, 1981, says that the "news media in the U.S. reported that the President wears an armored vest which can be pierced only by a rifle bullet--a Springfield 303, in the case of President Ford. What public purpose is served by telling a would-be-assassin that if he wants to kill the President, he should get a rifle, not a pistol?"

Sub-point B. Reporters are endangered when they cover live terrorist acts. Jullian Becker in *The PLO*, 1984, gives a good example of this. He writes,

> Salim al-Lawzi, owner and editor of an independent weekly newspaper, which warned in the early 1970's that the PLO was destructive to Lebanese unity, was seized by SKa'igua, carried off to the PLO-occupied mountain

village of Armun, and tortured to death. His body was found with the fingers cut off, apparently joint by joint, the eyes gorged out, and the limbs hacked off . . .

Clearly, this example proves that the media needs to be protected from themselves.

Sub-point C. Media endangers terrorist victims. Grant Wardlaw, research criminologist at the Australian Institute of Criminology, in the book, *Political Terrorism*, gives an example of this. He writes,

> The most damaging case concerned the TV reporter who caught sight of a basket lifted up by rope to the fifth floor where, the world later learned, some people evaded the round-up and barricaded themselves in a room. Their presence apparently was not known to the gunmen, who held their prisoners on the eighth floor but patrolled the lower floors until late Wednesday afternoon. The gunmen were probably informed of the TV report's scoop by fellow Hanafis who monitored the news media outside the captured buildings. Fortunately, the gunmen did not break through the door.

As you can see, the media are, indeed, feckless, and they present a clear and present danger to U.S. citizens. Therefore, significant restrictions on U.S. media coverage of terrorist acts are justified.

———————

This affirmative case was written, in the Fall of 1985, by Cindi Sellinger and Dorise Gray, members of the CSU, Chico debate team. Using this case, Cindi and Dorise placed first with an undefeated record at the Modesto Invitational, November 1985, in a competitive novice division of 14 teams.

APPENDIX B
VALUE OBJECTION

Value Objection Number I Internationalism is a superior value to U.S. national interests in the United Nations.

> **Sub-point A.** This debate concerns how we should value our membership in the United Nations. Our membership can be considered in two ways:
>
> > **Little 1.** As a mere vehicle of our national interests and foreign policy objectives, or
> >
> > **Little 2.** As a truly international body with interests which supersede those of individual member status.
>
> **Sub-point B.** In the United Nations, international concerns take precedence over national selfish interests.
>
> > **Little 1.** It is unfair, illogical and unrealistic to place the burden on the United Nations of having to meet the foreign policy objectives of all member states which the affirmative suggests as a value in sub-points _____ *[to be filled in with specific sub-point numbers and letters from 1AC]*.
> >
> > **Little 2.** Our expectations of the U.N. are too exaggerated when seen from the myopic view point of national interests.
>
> **Sub-point C.** Internationalism is a good value.
>
> > **Little 1.** We live in an interdependent world. According to *Toward a World Human Order* by Gerald and Patricia Mische, Professors of the Center for Humanistic Studies at Seaton Hall University,

The interdependencies between nations leave them vulnerable in multiple ways: A nuclear attack anywhere affects the whole species. Depletion of the ozone leaves all vulnerable to skin cancer. The pollution of the oceans and resulting destruction of oxygen-producing phytoplankton means less oxygen for us all. The devaluation of the American dollar while it can be undertaken unilaterally, affects global economic security. An increase of cost in Arab oil increases inflation everywhere, affecting the capacity of people to provide for their basic needs. A unilateral decision by one nation to change the flow of a river within its boundaries would vitally affect the security of the neighboring states also dependent on that river. The list is endless. In short, all nations are vulnerable to the decisions and actions of the world.

Thus, as the evidence indicates, our world is clearly interdependent.

Little 2. There are many vital world concerns which we share in common with other nations. Gerald and Patricia Mische, cited above, state,

There is now no choice but that our security be ensured in institutions that are global and that are built on a commonly shared sense of the interdependence of all who inhabit this one earth.

Little 3. The United Nations is the only truly international organization where common problems can be pursued in a shared sense of interdependence. Seymour Finger and Joseph Harbert in their book, *U.S. Policy in International Institutions*, 1982, explain,

The 1970's have witnessed a relatively new development in international institutions: patterns of increased use of *ad hoc* international conferences under U.N. auspices to deal with issues of global concern. Major conferences of food, water, population, human settlements, law of sea, the human environment and deserts have been held, and others are planned. One of the themes that ties these conferences together is the somewhat belated recognition that contemporary world problems are interrelated. This rise of global consciousness has stimulated the creation of a new world agenda, one which stresses common interests, interdependence and human survival.

Sub-point D. These myopic pursuits of national interest are a bad value. They promote a paranoia that turns national defense efforts into military excursions. Past wars have been caused by the pursuit of national interests, and, unless we do something now, future wars may soon follow.

Little 1. These myopic pursuits are said to have been the cause of our two world wars. From Abraham Yeselson and Anthony Goglione in their book, *A Dangerous Place*, 1974, they write, "World War One it was believed, could have been avoided if the great powers had been organized to confer before the crisis had reached a point of no return." And of the Second World War, George Schultz, secretary of state under Reagan, tells us in *The Secretary*, August 1985 that

Americans, in particular, recalled sadly that their country's retreat into isolation after that first great war was in no small measure to blame for the eruption of the second. The phrase on the lips of all Americans and all peoples everywhere was, "It must not happen again."

Little 2. National interests often contradict genuine international concerns. Gerald and Patricia Mische, as cited earlier, explain,

Excessive individualism in the formulation of national policies mitigates against the best long-range interest of its own citizenry as well as the interest of the human community.

Little 3. Failure to achieve internationalism will be disastrous. This prediction was made in the book, *Nuclear Power and Nuclear Weapon Proliferation*, written by the Atlantic Council of the United States, 1977; it says, "International cooperation is therefore indispensable to policies aimed at minimizing the extent and delaying the timing of any further proliferation." Further documentation for this point comes from Paul and Anne Erlich, professors of Biological Science at Stanford University, in their book, *Extinction*, 1981:

It is likely that destruction of the rich complex of species in the Amazon basin could trigger rapid changes in global climate, and human beings remain heavily dependent on food. By the end of the century, the extinction of perhaps a million species in the Amazon basin could have entrained famine in which a billion human beings perished. And if our species is very unlucky, the famine could lead to a thermal-nuclear war, which could extinguish civilization.

A logical outgrowth of selfish nationalism is a nuclear war to protect national interests. In establishing a hierarchy of values, internationalism must reign superior, for all our sakes.

This value objection was argued by Kimberly Horan and Tamara Hatcher at the 1986 C.E.D.A. National Tournament, in which they placed fifth in Novice Division. They won three out of four negative rounds using this argument. The resolution read, "Resolved: that membership in the United Nations is no longer beneficial to the United States."

APPENDIX C
HOW TO TAKE A
FLOW-SHEET

DEFINITION AND SET-UP

A flow-sheet, as the name indicates, is a record of the flow of arguments in a debate. An argument is traced from when it is first presented until its conclusion.

Begin with either a legal tablet 8 1/2 x 14 inches or preferably a large art pad. Divide the pad into the number of columns needed for the speeches you must record. For example, negative speakers do not need a place to record the last affirmative rebuttal. Also, do not include a place for the second negative constructive, which is recorded on a separate sheet.

A typical **on-case** flow-sheet should look likes this:

1AC	1NC	2AC	1NR	1AR	2NR	2AR

The **off-case** arguments (value objections) and responses to them are recorded on a separate set of paper. This is where the second negative constructive is recorded, as well as those portions of the first affirmative rebuttal, second negative rebuttal, and second affirmative rebuttals which deal with off-case arguments.

A typical off-case flow-sheet looks like this:

2NC	1AR	2NR	2AR

It is advisable to leave plenty of room (vertically) between arguments. Often a team will have multiple responses to one point of their opponents (this is known as spread debating). If you cramp yourself into a small amount of space per argument, it becomes nearly impossible to flow the debate. This is also why art pads are the preferred method of note-taking among beginning debaters.

FLOWING AN ARGUMENT

Below is an example of how an argument might progress through the constructive speeches into the first negative rebuttal. This argument might well continue through the remaining three speeches.

1st Affirmative	1st Negative	2nd Affirmative	1st Neg. Rebuttal
I. PROPERTY TAXES ARE REGRESSIVE *Maxwell 1992* "take from poor"	**I.** STATES MOVING AWAY FROM P.T. *Bk of sts. 1990* "41 have inc. tax"	**I.** 1) % OF P.T. REV. IS HIGH *Census 1991* 2) FED INC TAX PRE-EMPTS STS. *Ced '93*	**I.** 1)TREND IS NOT P.T. *Pechman 1991* 2) PRE-EMPT SIGNIF. *Jones 1992*

WHAT TO RECORD

First, label the argument. This would be the main heading, such as, "Property taxes are regressive."

Second, record the source and date. Although some would argue this is of secondary importance, some mention should be made, even if just of name and date.

Thus, qualifications and recency of evidence might well become decisive issues in the debate.

Finally, include quotations from parts of the evidence. This is just as important as the label itself. Why are property taxes regressive? In order to respond to an argument, you must be aware of its substance. In addition, it is not uncommon for a debate team to claim a quotation proves more than it actually says. Recording the substance of the evidence will help you catch such tactics. For instance, a team's claim may be in the realm of certainty, but the actual quotation says "perhaps." In such a case, you should write "perhaps" on your flow-sheet next to the argument. Thus, you can make an issue of it later.

HELPFUL HINTS

1. Never, never, never allow assertions to go unsubstantiated. It doesn't matter how apparent the point is, if there is any way it could be otherwise, ask for evidence. If an unsupported assertion is used, write "no ev" on your flow-sheet and push the point.

2. As an affirmative, you should have your case already outlined on a piece of paper you clip over the first column. Leave plenty of room between arguments. Your outline should be complete down to the evidence: This will help you stay organized.

3. Draw arrows from points in each speech to the same points in the next. If you answer more than one argument with the same point, use a bracket to indicate that these arguments have been "grouped" together.

4. Use two colors of pen: one for your arguments and one for your opponents'.

5. Develop a shorthand; don't write everything out. Thus, for example, F. G. = federal government.

6. When an argument is not answered (dropped), place a large X on your flow-sheet, or write "drop." Then, make sure you tell the judge that the opposition has dropped an argument, and, therefore, it is yours. Also, be sure to give impact to dropped arguments. In other words, tell your critic why the "drop" is critical in the debate.

7. When the opposition shifts from one position to another, write "shift," and tell the judge what happened. Shifting positions is a common tactic and often goes unnoticed unless it is pointed out.

HOW TO SPEAK FROM A FLOW-SHEET

A carefully taken flow-sheet can be a great help in staying organized. Failure to take a proper flow-sheet is probably the single greatest cause of disorganization. Start at the top of the flow-chart and work down. Be sure to signpost. In other words, tell the critic which argument you are addressing. Be specific and include the numbers and letters of the outline. If you move from contention IA to IB, say, "Turning now to point B," or words to that effect. If your opponents aren't organized, ORGANIZE THEM!

A good flow-sheet helps you summarize an argument as it has developed. Reading from left to right, you can follow the argument from its introduction to its current status. Be sure to tell the judge where you are, what the argument is, how the argument stands now, what your response is and then present your evidence and reasoning to support your point. For example:

> We originally argued in *Contention I sub-point A* that the Constitutional checks on the President are sufficient. They argued that the president is too powerful. My answer is, first of all, that they failed to respond to my analysis. . .

When taking a flow-sheet, be sure to listen to the date and source. Check to see whether the evidence really says what your opponent says it does. Finally, look for contradictions. Remember, adequate flow-sheeting can make the difference in a debate. Inadequate flow-sheeting can be devastating. Try to practice as often as you can: when other students or team members are debating, *etc*. And use the worksheets on the next few pages in this book.

FLOW-SHEET EXERCISES

The following pages include two flow-sheet exercises. The first exercise is easy. The second is more difficult. The first three pages of each exercise are three copies of a partial flow-sheet with the first column already charted for you. Have someone read the subsequent arguments aloud (or tape record them and play them back). As you listen, take a flow of the arguments using the techniques discussed here. Be sure to record the arguments in the proper column. If you plan to sell the book back at the end of the semester, please photo copy the worksheets and complete the exercises on the copies.

Dr. Steve Brydon, California State University, Chico, contributed significantly to the content of *appendix C*.

FLOWSHEET EXERCISE NUMBER ONE
Copy #1

The 1AC flow here represents arguments in favor of the resolution: "Resolved: That U.S. covert operations are undesirable."   Following three copies of this worksheet, you will find a text of the 1NC responses. Please have a classmate, using a separate book, read those responses aloud while you practice taking a flow-sheet. You may also tape record the responses and play them back. Try to follow the format above and be sure to record responses in the correct columns and rows (1NC responses in the 1NC column; sub-point A responses directly next to the sub-point A arguments from the previous column, and so on). Realize that this exercise does not represent an entire speech, but only a single contention. Also realize that a normal flow-sheet continues to the right of 1NC to include 2AC, 1NR, 1AR, 2NR, and 2AR. This flow-sheet is for the purpose of practice only. This worksheet is repeated twice for your convenience.

1AC   1NC

Contention I
All covert operations are bad.

Sub-point A.
Covert operations are
immoral.

Johnson 1989

"Murder and Lying"

Sub-point B.
U.S. backed rebels throughout
the world use torture

Benson 1990

"Tortured to death"

Sub-point C.
The governments we
attempt to overthrow are just.

Jefferson 1990

"Nicaragua a just government."

FLOWSHEET EXERCISE NUMBER ONE
Copy #2

The 1AC flow here represents arguments in favor of the resolution: "Resolved: That U.S. covert operations are undesirable." Following three copies of this worksheet, you will find a text of the 1NC responses. Please have a classmate, using a separate book, read those responses aloud while you practice taking a flow-sheet. You may also tape record the responses and play them back. Try to follow the format above and be sure to record responses in the correct columns and rows (1NC responses in the 1NC column; sub-point A responses directly next to the sub-point A arguments from the previous column, and so on). Realize that this exercise does not represent an entire speech, but only a single contention. Also realize that a normal flow-sheet continues to the right of 1NC to include 2AC, 1NR, 1AR, 2NR, and 2AR. This flow-sheet is for the purpose of practice only. This worksheet is repeated twice for your convenience.

1AC   1NC

Contention I
All covert operations are bad.

Sub-point A.
Covert operations are
immoral.

Johnson 1989

"Murder and Lying"

Sub-point B.
U.S. backed rebels throughout
the world use torture

Benson 1990

"Tortured to death"

Sub-point C.
The governments we
attempt to overthrow are just.

Jefferson 1990

"Nicaragua a just government.'

FLOWSHEET EXERCISE NUMBER ONE
Copy #3

The 1AC flow here represents arguments in favor of the resolution: "Resolved: That U.S. covert operations are undesirable."   Following three copies of this worksheet, you will find a text of the 1NC responses. Please have a classmate, using a separate book, read those responses aloud while you practice taking a flow-sheet. You may also tape record the responses and play them back. Try to follow the format above and be sure to record responses in the correct columns and rows (1NC responses in the 1NC column; sub-point A responses directly next to the sub-point A arguments from the previous column, and so on). Realize that this exercise does not represent an entire speech, but only a single contention. Also realize that a normal flow-sheet continues to the right of 1NC to include 2AC, 1NR, 1AR, 2NR, and 2AR. This flow-sheet is for the purpose of practice only. This worksheet is repeated twice for your convenience.

1AC   1NC

Contention I
All covert operations are bad.

Sub-point A.
Covert operations are
immoral.

Johnson 1989

"Murder and Lying"

Sub-point B.
U.S. backed rebels throughout
the world use torture

Benson 1990

"Tortured to death"

Sub-point C.
The governments we
attempt to overthrow are just.

Jefferson 1990

"Nicaragua a just government."

RESPONSES FOR FLOWSHEET EXERCISE NUMBER ONE, COPIES 1, 2, AND 3

FIRST NEGATIVE CONSTRUCTIVE--CONTENTION 1 ONLY

In **contention one**, my opponents argue that all covert operations are bad. I say that covert operations are necessary. Gregory F. Treverton, of the School of Government, at Harvard University, in *Foreign Affairs*, writing in the Summer of 1987, says,

> In this context, a unilateral self-denying ordinance against all intervention-- open or covert--is too restrictive. Some threats to American national security require responses. Some American friends in the Third World deserve support.

Therefore, covert operations are not bad, but necessary.

In **contention one, sub-point** A, my opponent argued that covert operations are immoral. I argue that the maintenance or establishment of freedom and individual rights is more important than a temporary lapse in morality. Charles Krauthammer, senior editor of *The New Republic*, in *Current* magazine, February 1987, explains:

> I accept the World Court's view that there are higher principles than non-intervention and higher values than order. The real moral question is: What are those higher values? I would accept decolonization as one, but would generalize it to read freedom, meaning a regime of democratic rule and individual rights, or, where that is not possible (Afghanistan, for example), of national independence and the relative freedom of living under a traditional government rather than under communism.

The impact of Krauthammer's argument suggests that intervention is moral because it results in the securing or maintenance of a democratic, or at least autonomous, *status quo*.

In **contention one, sub-point** B, my opponent reads evidence telling us that U.S. backed rebels use torture. We argue that the use of torture is inevitable but can be controlled. Krauthammer in 1987 again:

> By abuses, I mean terror and torture. If these are committed by members of an armed force, its cause is not necessarily de-legitimized. These abuses always occur. The important question is whether or not the use of such means is deliberate policy, and whether the army, guerrilla or otherwise, establishes rules prohibiting such conduct and takes steps to enforce the rules.

The important question, then, as Krauthammer explains, is not whether torture occurs, but whether the rebels are trying to avoid the abuses. The affirmative fails to address motives at all.

In **contention one, sub-point** C, they argued that the governments we attempt to overthrow are benevolent. We argue that the governments we try to overthrow are repressive. We'll also use the example of the Nicaragua Sandanistas. James H. Michel,

Deputy Asst. Secretary of State under Reagan, in the *Department of State Bulletin*, August 1986, explains:

> And the Sandinistas have engaged in increasingly severe repression of the voices of dissent--in the church, the labor movement, political parties, the business community, and the press. They seek consolidation of a system of party control and are determined to crush their opposition.

So, obviously, the Sandinistas are repressive, not benevolent as the Affirmative would have you believe.

FLOWSHEET EXERCISE NUMBER TWO
Copy #1

The 1AC flow here corresponds with the affirmative case in *Appendix A* of this book. Following three copies of this worksheet, you will find a text of the 1NC and 2AC responses. Please have a classmate, using a separate book, read those responses aloud while you practice taking a flow-sheet. Try to follow the format above and be sure to record responses in the correct columns and rows (1NC responses in the 1NC column; sub-point A responses directly next to the sub-point A arguments from the previous column, and so on). Realize that this exercise does not represent an entire speech, but only a single contention. Also realize that a normal flow-sheet continues to the right of 2AC to include 1NR, 1AR, 2NR, and 2AR. This flow-sheet is for the purpose of practice only. This worksheet is repeated twice for your convenience.

1AC	1NC	2AC
Contention III The media is feckless.		
Sub-point A. Media gives away important information. *Elkins 1981* Pres. Armored vest		
Sub-point B. Reporters lives endangered. *Jullian Becker 1984* tortured to death		
Sub-point C. Media endangers hostages. *Wardlaw, Political Terrorism* T.V. revealed hostages' locale		

FLOWSHEET EXERCISE NUMBER TWO
Copy #2

The 1AC flow here corresponds with the affirmative case in *Appendix A* of this book. Following three copies of this worksheet, you will find a text of the 1NC and 2AC responses. Please have a classmate, using a separate book, read those responses aloud while you practice taking a flow-sheet. Try to follow the format above and be sure to record responses in the correct columns and rows (1NC responses in the 1NC column; sub-point A responses directly next to the sub-point A arguments from the previous column, and so on). Realize that this exercise does not represent an entire speech, but only a single contention. Also realize that a normal flow-sheet continues to the right of 2AC to include 1NR, 1AR, 2NR, and 2AR. This flow-sheet is for the purpose of practice only. This worksheet is repeated twice for your convenience.

1AC	1NC	2AC
Contention III The media is feckless.		
Sub-point A. Media gives away important information. *Elkins 1981* Pres. Armored vest		
Sub-point B. Reporters lives endangered. *Jullian Becker 1984* tortured to death		
Sub-point C. Media endangers hostages. *Wardlaw, Political Terrorism* T.V. revealed hostages' locale		

FLOWSHEET EXERCISE NUMBER TWO
Copy #3

The 1AC flow here corresponds with the affirmative case in *Appendix A* of this book. Following three copies of this worksheet, you will find a text of the 1NC and 2AC responses. Please have a classmate, using a separate book, read those responses aloud while you practice taking a flow-sheet. Try to follow the format above and be sure to record responses in the correct columns and rows (1NC responses in the 1NC column; sub-point A responses directly next to the sub-point A arguments from the previous column, and so on). Realize that this exercise does not represent an entire speech, but only a single contention. Also realize that a normal flow-sheet continues to the right of 2AC to include 1NR, 1AR, 2NR, and 2AR. This flow-sheet is for the purpose of practice only. This worksheet is repeated twice for your convenience.

1AC	1NC	2AC

Contention III
The media is feckless.

Sub-point A.
Media gives away
important information.

Elkins 1981

Pres. Armored vest

Sub-point B.
Reporters lives endangered.

Jullian Becker 1984

tortured to death

Sub-point C.
Media endangers hostages.

Wardlaw, Political Terrorism

T.V. revealed hostages' locale

RESPONSES FOR FLOWSHEET EXERCISE NUMBER TWO, COPIES 1, 2, AND 3

FIRST NEGATIVE CONSTRUCTIVE--CONTENTION 3 ONLY

In terms of **contention three**, the media are feckless, no evidence was provided, so I will simply respond by saying that, on the whole, media are responsible.

In terms of **contention three, sub-point A**, they argue that the media give away information. We say that the media double check information before they broadcast it. Mr. Siegenthaler, Vice President of ABC, as quoted in *Broadcasting* magazine, August 5th, 1985, gives us an example of this:

> ABC denied the terrorist uncontrolled access. All interviews and statements from Beirut, telecast by ABC, with one exception were pre-taped and edited by us.

Therefore, the media do not just give away important information.

In terms of **contention three, sub-point B**, they argue that reporters are endangered. We argue that that's part of their job and part of the risks they must take. There are risks with any job. I challenge the affirmative to prove that the risk to reporters is significant. This evidence only gives one example of one reporter. I think we have a fallacy of example argument on our hands. This is an insufficient and atypical example; thus, the affirmative must loose this point.

In terms of **contention three, sub-point C**, they argue that media endanger hostages' lives. First response is that again we have a fallacy of example argument. Their claim is a general statement, but they only give one insufficient and atypical example. Additionally, the example is irrelevant because no harm occurred to the hostages. The terrorists knew where the people were and didn't do anything. Therefore, the argument is weak, very weak. Second response is that the media often help the hostages. Stephen Gladis, of the FBI, in *The Hostage-Terrorist Situation and the Media*, U.S. Department of Justice, 1984:

> The police and media in such hostage-terrorist situations need not be antagonists. In fact, the news media at different times has helped resolve the hostage taker's demands. Such was the case in Cleveland when a police captain and a 17-year-old-female employee of the police department were taken hostage in 1977. The hostage taker refused to talk to police negotiators and would only discuss his situation with a local black television reporter. Under the guidance of police, the reporter talked the hostage taker out of the situation, and no one was injured.

Therefore, the media actually help instead of hinder the situation.

SECOND AFFIRMATIVE CONSTRUCTIVE--CONTENTION 3 ONLY

In **contention three**, we originally argued that the media are feckless. My opponents responded with the original, "the media are responsible." Our position is that the media may be responsible some of the time or even much of the time, but we must protect ourselves from the devastatingly harmful times when they present a clear and present danger.

In **contention three, sub-point A**, we originally argued that the media give away harmful information. Our opponents said the media double-check information before they release it. First response, later our opponents accuse us of using atypical examples.

Well, they seem to be violating their own standard here. This ABC thing is atypical and insufficient. Second response on contention three, sub-point A, their evidence is inconsistent within itself. Their own evidence even says that there was "one exception" to ABC's strict editorial control. Well, what if that one time was enough to cause the death of a hostage? The ABC example is an affirmative example because it proves the media are feckless and inconsistent. Third response, remember our 1AC evidence: an empirical example of media giving away unnecessary but harmful information about the president's vest. People don't need to know this trivial information. Yet it threatens lives. Fourth response, another example involves live T.V. interviews. Evidence comes from Juanita Jones and Abraham Miller, professors of poly sci at the University of Cincinnati, in the *Ohio Northern University Law Review*, January 1979.

> On too many occasions the media have held live interviews over the airways with terrorists who were holding hostages. In such situations a slip of the tongue, a poorly chosen phrase, or an intonation that rings of dissonance can have tragic consequences.

Another instance of media irresponsibility. Do I see a preponderance of evidence building here?

Sub-point B, we originally argued in 1AC that reporters are endangered. They argued insignificant and atypical. We argue that we don't have to prove that every reporter is endangered. Our society protects workers in other occupations: factory workers, farm workers, and so on. We should also protect reporters.

Sub-point C, we originally argued that the media endanger hostages lives. Their first response was fallacy of example argument. We are not arguing the media are always feckless. We are arguing that they are inconsistent and therefore cause a clear and present danger. Their first response also said our example was irrelevant because nothing happened to the hostages. However, our position is not that people have to die, but that a clear and present danger is created by the presence of the media. This example clearly shows us that. Their second response was that media often help hostages. However, in their example, the reporter worked for the police, not as a reporter. Had the other media reported that he was a police representative, he may have died instead of saved the day. In extension of sub-point C, we argue that overall this is a problem. From, Jones and Miller, 1979, cited earlier,

> The intrusion of journalists can affect the situation adversely; often placing the lives of hostages in jeopardy. Yet this happens all too often. Reporters have tied up phone lines making it impossible for negotiations to begin or they have broadcast details of police procedure thus providing the perpetrators with useful tactical knowledge.

Clearly, this is a problem, as Jones and Miller suggest.

APPENDIX D
RESEARCH AND
EVIDENCE

EVIDENCE ASSIGNMENT

Normally, your instructor or debate coach will assign you to find a certain number of quotations or to research a certain angle on the national C.E.D.A. topic (or other non-policy topic). Research is viewed often as a team effort, and each member will be asked to carry a certain part of the load. If needed, avail yourself to a tour of your school's library, or have a coach or senior debater demonstrate how to use some of the key indexes, such as *The Congressional Information Service.*

WHAT TO RECORD

Evidence can be broadly divided into two categories: **fact** and **opinion**. Within these categories, a number of individual types of evidence can be found. Some common types of **factual evidence** include the following:

Statements of condition: "Soldiers missing in action from the Vietnam War are still alive."
Examples: "The murder of Marines in Lebanon and the escalation of our role in the Persian Gulf are examples of Presidents abusing their role as civilian military leader."
Statistics: "Over 50% of Americans are over the age of 30."

Opinion evidence can cover a wide variety of possibilities:

Statements of Cause and Effect: "Increased military spending directly harms the economic machinery."

Statements of value: "It is better to have a weak President than strong one."
Statements advocating a policy: "We should have greater checks on the power of the Presidency."

There are other types of fact and opinion evidence, but this will give you an idea of the variety of proof that you can find. Most often, you will want to include the reasoning or analysis behind the conclusion as well as the conclusion. Opinion evidence varies in value based on the expertise of your source, the degree of bias (if any), and the soundness of the reasoning. For statistical information, try to find the methodology of the study as well as the conclusion to it. Study indictments are common in intercollegiate debating, and knowing the way the study was done is invaluable when defending your evidence against attacks.

HOW MUCH TO RECORD

The most common error among beginning debaters is to record too much or too little. If the quotations are too long, you may have a problem with time-limits in a debate. A quotation that takes a minute to read may prove your point, but it may cost you two or three other points. Keep quotations brief, to the point, while retaining the intended context. On the other hand, failing to record enough of a quotation often causes problems as well. A single conclusionary sentence rarely wins a debate round or an argument. Try to keep your evidence around two to three sentences average. Be sure to include the analysis that supports the conclusion. Factual evidence may be fine as one sentence. More complex evidence may need to be four or five sentences.

FORMAT FOR RECORDING

While different individuals may have different systems, in collective research it is important that everyone use the same format. The following format is fairly standard. Include the name of the person, his or her most significant credentials, title of the book or periodical, complete date, and page number(s). Put your initials at the end of the quotation, so that, if a colleague has a question, he or she can ask you.

```
Name, Qualifications, Title, Date, Page(s)




                    QUOTATION




                                  Y.I. (Your Initials)
```

It is not necessary to put a heading on the quotation, since each individual should do this for him or herself when filing evidence. Also, contrary to the recommendation of some textbooks, citations should be at the top of the quotation, since you always read this before reading the quotation.

SAMPLE EVIDENCE FORMAT

The following is what your evidence should look like after you type it. Be sure to indent or leave a space between the source citation and the evidence quotation.

J. Phillip Wogeman, professor of Christian Social Ethics at Wesley Theological Seminary, in *The American Academy of Political and Social Science Annals*, November 1979, p. XXX
    And religious groups, when they go lobbying for [their own theological views], must expect them to be struck down eventually by the courts even if they are enacted into law.   jmc

---

The evidence need not be typed directly onto an index card, but it should be able to fit on a standard 4 x 6 card. Usually, an argumentation class or a debate team will specify how to compile the data. This information is provided simply to get you started.

Dr. Steve Brydon, California State University, Chico, contributed significantly to the content of *appendix D*.

GLOSSARY

Affirmative: A debater or debate team that supports a particular proposition. For example, on the proposition, "Resolved: that continued military involvement in the Persian Gulf area would be undesirable," affirmative arguments would support that statement. In other words, the affirmative debater answers "yes" to the question implied by the proposition, "Is military involvement undesirable?"

Argumentation: The justification of facts, values, beliefs, or policies through oral or written advocacy. Also, the theory used to evaluate such advocacy.

Burden of Proof: A necessity to prove an assertion. Affirmative teams are required to demonstrate the desirability or validity of their proposed fact, value, or policy.

Case: The arguments chosen by an affirmative team to support a given resolution. Those arguments are presented in an eight-to-ten minute speech as the first order of business in a debate round. In the course of a debate, advocates refer to those affirmative arguments as *case, case side, on case*, or *the affirmative case.*

C.E.D.A.: An acronym for *Cross Examination Debate Association*, the intercollegiate debate organization that sponsors non-policy debate topics.

Constructives: In team debate, the first four speeches in which advocates build arguments for and against the resolution and against each other. In non-policy debate, those speeches are usually eight minutes long.

Contention: An extended argument supporting an advocate's position. A contention usually contains at least two different pieces of evidence in support of an issue. Debate contentions are delivered in outline form, and each sub-point in the outline is supported by evidence.

Counterwarrants: General resolutional attacks by the negative. Rather than link arguments to the affirmative position, the negative instead refutes various examples of or warrants for the resolution. The negative usually justifies counterwarrants by demonstrating that the affirmative interpretation of the resolution is in some way unreasonable or narrow.

Debate: Academic debating involves extensive research on a resolution and advocacy of both affirmative and negative positions. Advocates attempt to persuade a third party, usually a debate coach or speech instructor, that their arguments are superior.

Definitive Contention: An argument or series of arguments in which the affirmative attempts to establish the standard, value, or criterion for a particular resolutional interpretation. A definitive contention may or may not involve specific definitions of terms.

Designative Contention: Affirmative arguments in a non-policy debate that evaluate an issue based on the standards or values set in the definitive contention.

Forensics: Intercollegiate speech and debate competition.

N.D.T.: *National Debate Tournament* is an annual tournament (and activity) sponsored by the American Forensic Association that traditionally uses propositions of policy.

Negative: Negative teams or advocates usually refute the affirmative case and offer constructive arguments that deny the validity of the resolution.

Non-Policy Debate: Consists of a formal educational activity in which two to four participants contend over propositions which are not policy-oriented or legislative in nature. Usually, non-policy debates dispute the nature and application of values (values such as freedom and the sanctity of human life).

On-Case: In non-policy debate, the affirmative case and subsequent arguments for and against it. Also, *case side*.

Off-Case: In non-policy debate, the negative case, or value objections, (usually presented in second negative constructive) and subsequent arguments for and against.

Presumption: The assumption that the present system will remain in effect until desirable and sufficient reasons are found to change it. In non-policy debate, presumption is not well established but usually lies with the negative.

Rebuttals: Speeches in which advocates are expected to refute the most recent opposing arguments and rebuild their own position. Rebuttals should summarize constructive arguments and provide a clear focus for the debate.

Stock Issues: The standard arguments that must be proven by affirmative advocates.

SELECTED REFERENCES

Bartanen, M. D. (1982). The role of values in policy controversies. In Don Brownlee (Ed.), *C.E.D.A. Yearbook 1982* (pp. 19-24). Long Beach, CA: C.E.D.A.

Bartanen, M. D. (1988). *C.E.D.A. Report*. Tacoma, WA.

Best, J. A. (1980). *The mainstream of western political thought.* New York: Human Sciences Press.

Berube, M. (1984). Debating hasty generalizations. In Don Brownlee (Ed.), *C.E.D.A. Yearbook 1984* (pp. 54-59). Long Beach, CA: C.E.D.A.

Biggers, T. (1985). A single swallow and other leaps of faith. In Don Brownlee (Ed.), *C.E.D.A. Yearbook 1985* (pp. 32-38). Long Beach, CA: C.E.D.A.

Brey, J. (1989). A descriptive analysis of CEDA judging philosophies part I: Definitive acceptance or rejection of certain tactics and arguments. In Walter Ulrich (Ed.), *CEDA Yearbook* (pp. 67-77). Dubuque: Kendall/Hunt.

Brownlee, D. (1980). Advocacy and values. In Don Brownlee (Ed.), *Perspectives on Non-Policy Argument* (pp. 43-47). Long Beach, CA: C.E.D.A.

Brownlee, D. (1981). In search of topicality. In Don Brownlee, (Ed.), *Contributions on the Philosophy and Practice of C.E.D.A.* (pp. 32-35), Long Beach, CA: C.E.D.A.

Brownlee, D. (1982). Debating value propositions. In Carolyn Keefe, Thomas B. Harte, Laurence Norton. (Eds.), *Introduction to Debate.* (pp. 287-292). New York: McMillan.

Brownlee, D. (1982). The consequences of quantification. In Don Brownlee, (Ed.), *C.E.D.A. Yearbook 1982* (pp. 29-31). Long Beach, CA: C.E.D.A.

Brownlee, D. (1986). *C.E.D.A. Report #12,* Long Beach, CA.

Brydon, S. R. (1984). Judging C.E.D.A. debate: a systems perspective.   In Don
    Brownlee, (Ed.), *C.E.D.A. Yearbook 1984* (pp. 85-88). Long Beach, CA: C.E.D.A.

Brydon, S. R. (1986). Presumption in non-policy debate: In search of a paradigm.
    Journal of the American Forensic Association, 23, 15-22.

Church, R. T., Wilbanks, C. (1986). *Values and policies in controversy: An introduction
    to argumentation and debate.* Scottsdale: Gorsuch Scarisbrick.

Cirlin, A. (1984). On negative strategy in value debate. In Don Brownlee, (Ed.),
    C.E.D.A. Yearbook 1984 (pp. 31-39). Long Beach, CA: C.E.D.A.

Cirlin, A. (1986). Evaluating cross-examination in C.E.D.A. debate: On getting our act
    together. In Brenda Logue (Ed.), *1986 Yearbook Cross Examination Debate
    Association* (pp. 43-50). Towson, MD: C.E.D.A.

Darley, J. M., Gross, P. H. (1981). A hypothesis-confirming bias in labeling effect.
    Journal of Personality and Social Psychology, 28.

Dixon, T. S., Leslie, C. R. (1984). Propositional analysis: A need for focus in C.E.D.A.
    debate. In Don Brownlee (Ed.), *C.E.D.A. Yearbook 1984* (pp. 16-23). Long Beach,
    CA: C.E.D.A.

Ehninger, D., Brockriede, W. (1963). *Decision by debate.* Toronto: Dodd, Mead, and
    Company.

Ehninger, D., Brockriede, W. (1978). *Decision by debate.* New York: Harper and Row.

Eisenberg, A. M., Llardo, J. A. (1980). *Argument: A guide to formal and informal
    debate.* New Jersey: Prentice-Hall.

Freeley, A. J. (1981). *Argumentation and debate: Reasoned decision making.* Belmont:
    Wadsworth publishing.

Freeley, A. J. (1986). *Argumentation and debate: Critical thinking for reasoned decision
    making.* Belmont: Wadsworth Publishing.

Fryar, M., and Thomas, D. A. (1979). *Basic debate.* Skokie, IL: National.

Gergen, K. J., Gergen, M. M. (1981). *Social psychology.* New York: Harcourt.

Gross, W., (1984). A case for debating propositions of policy. In Don Brownlee (Ed.),
    C.E.D.A. Yearbook 1984 (pp. 7-10). Long Beach, CA: C.E.D.A.

Henderson, B. (1980). Theoretical implications of debating non-policy propositions. In
    Don Brownlee (Ed.), *Perspectives on Non-Policy Argument* (pp. 1-12). Long Beach,
    CA: C.E.D.A.

Howe, J. H. (1981). C.E.D.A.s objectives; lest we forget. In Don Brownlee (Ed.),
    Contributions on the Philosophy and Practice of C.E.D.A. (pp. 1-3). Long Beach, CA:
    C.E.D.A.

Howe, J. H. (1982). Debate should be a laughing matter. In Don   Brownlee (Ed.), *C.E.D.A. Yearbook 1982* (pp. 1-3). Long Beach, CA: C.E.D.A.

Howe, J. H. (1985). It's time for open season on squirrels. In Don Brownlee (Ed.), *C.E.D.A.Yearbook 1985* (pp. 14-20). Long Beach, CA: C.E.D.A.

Ingalls, Z. (1985). Resolved that competition in collegiate debate is as fierce as in a basketball play-off game. *The Chronicle of Higher Education, 29, 30*.

Jensen, V. J. (1981). *Argumentation: Reasoning in communication.* New York: D. Van Nostrand Company.

Jones, A. M., Crawford, S. W. (1984). Justification of values in terms of action. In Don Brownlee (Ed.), *C.E.D.A. Yearbook 1984* (pp. 11-14). Long Beach, CA: C.E.D.A.

Kahane, H. (1984). *Logic and contemporary rhetoric: The use of reason in everyday life.* Belmont: Wadsworth.

Kaplan, A. (1964). *The Conduct of Inquiry.* Chicago: Chandler.

Kelley, B. M. (1981). An alternative to N.D.T. debate. In Don Brownlee (Ed.), *Contributions on the Philosophy and Practice of C.E.D.A.* (pp. 8-14). Long Beach, CA: C.E.D.A.

Matlon, R. J. (1978). Debating propositions of value. *The Journal of the American Forensic Association. 14,* 198-204.

Matlon, R. J. (1988). Debating propositions of value: An idea revisited. In Brenda Logue (Ed.), *CEDA Yearbook* (pp. 1-14). Dubuque: Kendall/Hunt.

Miller, T. H., McVay, K. R. (1984). An audience analysis curriculum: Its theory, practice and implications. In Don Brownlee (Ed.), *C.E.D.A. Yearbook 1984* (pp. 65-73). Long Beach, CA: C.E.D.A.

Millsap, S., Millsap, S. (1985). Reflections on solvency in quasi-policy propositions. In Don Brownlee (Ed.), *C.E.D.A. Yearbook 1985* (pp. 29-31). Long Beach, CA: C.E.D.A.

Patterson, J. W., Zarefsky, D. (1983). *Contemporary debate.* Boston: Houghton Mifflin Company.

Podgurski, D. T. (1983). Presumption in the value proposition realm. In Don Brownlee (Ed.), *C.E.D.A. Yearbook 1983* (pp. 34-39). Long Beach, CA: C.E.D.A.

Ray, J., Zavos, H. (1966). Reasoning and argument: Deduction and induction. In Gerald R. Miller and Thomas R. Nilsen, (Eds.), *Perspectives on argumentation.* Chicago: Scott Foresman and Company.

Rieke, R. D., Sillars, M. O. (1984). *Argumentation and the decision making process.* Glenview: Scott, Foresmen and Company.

Rokeach, M. (1973). *The nature of human values.* New York: The Free Press.

Sanders, G. H. (1983). *Introduction to contemporary academic debate*. Prospect Heights: Waveland Press Inc.

Sayer, J. E. (1980). *Argumentation and debate: Principles and applications*. Sherman Oaks: Alfred Publishing Company.

Scott, R. J., Wynn, T. (1981). Avoidance of the false claim: Some considerations for debating and judging propositions of value. In Don Brownlee (Ed.), *Contributions on The Philosophy and Practice of C.E.D.A.* (pp. 20-31). Long Beach, CA: C.E.D.A.

Sheckels Jr., T. F. (1984). *Debating: Applied rhetorical theory*. New York and London: Longman.

Simon, J. E. (1980). *Argumentation and debate: Principles and applications*. Sherman Oaks: Alfred Publishing Company.

Sproule, J. M. (1976). The psychological burden of proof: On the evolution of Richard Whately's theory of presumption. *Communication Monographs. 43*, 115.

Sproule, J. M. (1980). *Argument, language and its influence*. New York: McGraw Hill.

Thompson, W. N. (1971). *Modern argumentation and debate: Principles and practices*. New York: Harper and Row.

Tolbert, G., Hunt, S. (1985). Counter warrants: A method for testing topical justification in C.E.D.A. debate. In Don Brownlee (Ed.), *C.E.D.A. Yearbook 1985* (pp. 21-28). Long Beach, CA: C.E.D.A.

Ulrich, W. (1983). Philosophical systems as paradigms for value debate. In Don Brownlee (Ed.), *C.E.D.A. Yearbook 1983* (pp. 22-28). Long Beach, CA: C.E.D.A.

Vasilius, J. (1980). Presumption, presumption, wherefore art thou presumption? In Don Brownlee (Ed.), *Perspectives on Non-Policy Argument.* (pp. 33-42). Long Beach, CA: C.E.D.A.

Whately, R. (1963). *The elements of rhetoric*, (Ed.) Douglas Ehninger, 7th ed. (p. 124) Carbondale: Southern Illinois University Press.

Whillock, R. K. (1988). The practice of theory: A controversy in current debate. *The Forensic of Pi Kappa Delta, 73*, 6-15.

Zeuschner, R., Hill, A. (1981). Psychological presumption: its place in value topic debate. In Don Brownlee (Ed.), *Contributions on the Philosophy and Practice of C.E.D.A.* (pp. 20-31). Long Beach, CA: C.E.D.A.

INDEX